LEADING FOR EQUALITY

Making Schools Fairer

SAGE was founded in 1965 by Sara Miller McCune to support the dissemination of usable knowledge by publishing innovative and high-quality research and teaching content. Today, we publish over 900 journals, including those of more than 400 learned societies, more than 800 new books per year, and a growing range of library products including archives, data, case studies, reports, and video. SAGE remains majority-owned by our founder, and after Sara's lifetime will become owned by a charitable trust that secures our continued independence.

Los Angeles | London | New Delhi | Singapore | Washington DC | Melbourne

LEADING FOR EQUALITY

Making Schools Fairer

JACKY LUMBY | MARIANNE COLEMAN

SAGE

Los Angeles | London | New Delhi
Singapore | Washington DC | Melbourne

Los Angeles | London | New Delhi
Singapore | Washington DC | Melbourne

SAGE Publications Ltd
1 Oliver's Yard
55 City Road
London EC1Y 1SP

SAGE Publications Inc.
2455 Teller Road
Thousand Oaks, California 91320

SAGE Publications India Pvt Ltd
B 1/I 1 Mohan Cooperative Industrial Area
Mathura Road
New Delhi 110 044

SAGE Publications Asia-Pacific Pte Ltd
3 Church Street
#10-04 Samsung Hub
Singapore 049483

Editor: Marianne Lagrange
Editorial assistant: Robert Patterson
Production editor: Tom Bedford
Copyeditor: Gemma Marren
Proofreader: Audrey Scriven
Marketing manager: Dilhara Attygalle
Cover design: Naomi Robinson
Typeset by: C&M Digitals (P) Ltd, Chennai, India
Printed and bound by CPI Group (UK) Ltd,
Croydon, CR0 4YY

Library of Congress Control Number: 2016935137

British Library Cataloguing in Publication data

A catalogue record for this book is available from the British Library

ISBN 978-1-4739-1628-9
ISBN 978-1-4739-1629-6 (pbk)

Contents

About the authors

Jacky Lumby is a Professor of Education at the University of Southampton. She joined higher education after a varied career in schools, with posts in London, rural Cumbria and Cardiff, and later in adult, community and further education. She also worked in a Training and Enterprise Council with a regional responsibility for the development of leaders in both business and education. She has researched and published widely on the leadership of schools and colleges in the UK, Ireland, China and South Africa, in particular exploring how educational leadership relates to equity and the inclusion of learners and staff. This has led her to engage with issues like socio-economic class, ethnicity, gender and power. She is concerned with learning how those in education can lead people and systems that offer success to pupils and staff in the context of living a life they value.

Marianne Coleman is Reader Emerita in Educational Leadership at University College London, Institute of Education. Before a career in higher education at the University of Leicester and the Institute of Education she was a secondary school teacher and an advisory teacher in an LEA. Now retired, she continues to research and write focusing on her interest in gender and leadership and wider issues of diversity and social justice. She has recently co-authored a book on ageing and is a trustee of the Nurture Group Network, an educational charity which supports children with social, emotional and behavioural difficulties.

Preface

Education can be a force for greater equality in our communities, enabling everyone to achieve more of their potential to the benefit of both individuals and society. However, it is easy to lose sight of this over-arching purpose in the day-to-day routine of classrooms, assessments and results. Leaders in schools would say that they aspire to enable the highest possible levels of achievement for all and that they aim to treat individuals fairly, but more than two decades of researching equality in schools has shown us that, for many learners, this is far from reality. In particular, those who differ from an assumed norm are the most likely to be overlooked and marginalized, to the detriment of their education.

The two of us have written previously on leadership and diversity in education when we engaged with theories and concepts to support practice (Lumby with Coleman, 2007). In this book we wanted a different focus: to look not just at what the concepts mean in the context of education, but also at how to put them into action. We have engaged with real schools, illustrating our discussions with instances of how they are working to make life fairer for students and staff. In each chapter, therefore, are examples of ways in which you might tackle some of the practical issues to make your school fairer.

The book is entitled *Leading for Equality: Making Schools Fairer* and is aimed at all who are in leadership roles. Our definition of leadership is broad, going beyond the head teacher/principal and the senior leadership team to encompass the department and subject head, the leadership of the teacher in the classroom, those leading in support roles, and touching on the potential leadership of learners. We chose to use the word 'equality' as shorthand for many related ideas: equity, inclusion, diversity and social justice. We feel that these moral concepts are of vital relevance today, as our societies become more diverse and communities struggle to unite in the face of many destabilizing challenges.

Over time, people are becoming more aware and respectful of the differences between individuals and groups, often with the benefit of legislation to protect individual rights. Despite such advances, lingering prejudices remain and there is still a tendency to regard the norm as White, middle-class, male, heterosexual and probably Christian, with all individuals and groups judged against this baseline. There is also a tendency to stereotype individuals on the basis of the group or groups to which they belong. In this book, we ask you to examine your individual stance and that taken by your school to probe the part you play in dismantling or strengthening inequality.

The fundamental point is to bring about change in schools, to make them fairer. This can only be achieved through you, the reader – your values, your aims, your actions. We hope that this book supports you and wish you well in your endeavours.

Acknowledgements

A book such as this is only possible with the help of many people. The varied illustrations of policy and practice that we have been able to include are the result of support from staff in schools in England, Scotland and Wales and other educators who generously shared their experience with us. Of necessity, they must remain anonymous, nevertheless we should like to express our gratitude at their openness and willingness to share. They were driven in all cases by a wish to contribute to the mission of increasing equality in our schools. We thank them all.

We would also like to thank Marianne Lagrange, Robert Patterson and Rachael Plant at Sage, for their support of this publication and ongoing ideas for its development. Alison Williamson undertook initial copyediting and proofing, and provided useful feedback.

Finally, we would like to thank the very many children and young people to whom we have spoken throughout twenty years of researching schools. Their stories and opinions have provided a constant reminder of the human experience at the heart of schooling, and have motivated us to continue researching and writing about equality.

Part I

The context and in/equality

1

Ideas of equality: The contested concept

In this opening chapter, we set out what the book as a whole is intended to achieve. We also provide initial ideas to help you reach a clearer understanding of what is implied by equality in education, and stimulate you to consider the relationship between equality and school practice in more detail.

In this chapter we ask you to think about:

- the aims and structure of the book
- what equality means in schools
- the range of language and concepts used in this area
- what various ideas about equality imply about aims.

Throughout the book we use case examples that help to illustrate the points being made. They are a convenience sample drawn from interviews with current head teachers and other leaders in state and private schools in England, Wales and Scotland. The structure of the education system is complex and varied in the four countries of the United Kingdom (UK), with types of school reflecting differing governance arrangements and degrees of autonomy. Our case examples are illustrative of the range, including academies, community, foundation and faith schools. A reference providing more detail about types of schools is given at the end of the chapter.

The names of the schools are pseudonyms, but we provide information about the age range, whether co-educational or single-sex, and the geographic location of each, as appropriate. The schools selected are generally those that were suggested to us as having responded to often challenging circumstances in interesting ways. The case examples are boxed so you can see clearly on the page where there are illustrations of practice. These are intended to encourage debate and enable you to reach your own conclusions about appropriate practice.

In this chapter, illustrative case examples are drawn from two co-educational schools in the south of England: Winburg Academy (11–18), and Elands Community School (11–16).

Aims of the book

For many, one particular story has come to summarize how education does not live up to ideals of equality. This is the parable in the Gospel of Matthew in the Bible that tells the story of a master who for safe-keeping gives ten bags of gold to one servant and only one bag to another. In his master's absence, the servant with ten bags uses enterprise to double the gold. He is praised by the master. The servant with one bag is so afraid of losing it that he buries it and then returns the single bag to his master, explaining that he has kept it safe. For this, the master punishes him and his gold is given to the servant who was initially given the most:

> The man who has will always be given more, till he has enough and to spare; and the man who has not will forfeit even what he has. (*Matthew* 25: 28–30, New Testament)

This parable has generated the phrase the 'Matthew effect', capturing the idea that those who have most can generally use it to get more. The 'Matthew effect' summarizes much of the impact of education worldwide. Those who come from an advantaged background often cluster together in schools, in ability groups, in universities and, ultimately, in jobs with prospects, and in influential social and political roles. Despite the widely held belief that education is a mechanism for achieving greater equality, evidence suggests the contrary is often the case (OECD, 2014a). We hope that through this book we can contribute to countering the 'Matthew effect' and help you to do the same.

An overview of the nature and scale of the problem is a good way to begin. It is salutary to recognize just how much inequality remains in education in the twenty-first century. For example, the 2015 Millennium Goal for all children to have a primary education has now been deferred until 2030

(Oxfam, 2010). Some might assume that attendance at school is primarily an issue for developing countries. This is not so. It is true that the scale of inequality may be much greater in developing economies, but even in the UK in autumn 2014 nearly 5 per cent of children were persistently absent (DfE, 2015a). Across the globe, for those who are in school, education generally reproduces socioeconomic divisions (Reay, 2010). Socioeconomic class is a relevant factor, but children's own accounts and statistical evidence attest to many other factors such as ethnicity or sexuality that should be irrelevant, but nevertheless relate to their being unhappy or unsuccessful at school (Hull et al., 2009; Reardon, 2011).

We would guess that you have started reading this book because you are interested in equality, but perhaps that does not quite cover it. Perhaps you are passionately committed to equality. Commitment is common, yet education systems remain unfair (Fair Education Alliance, 2014). This is the conundrum at the heart of this book: on the one hand, practitioners aiming at equality, and on the other, profoundly unequal education chances in many parts of the world. Despite the potential for education to transform children's lives, it is much more likely to do so for some groups of children than others.

Despite their commitment to equality, school leaders and teachers do not necessarily think through coherently what they aim to achieve and how. This book will help practitioners and especially leaders to clarify goals and alternative approaches, and to develop practice by considering values, attitudes, structures and pedagogy. The book does not offer definitive answers. These do not exist. It does however offer a challenge and ideas to find ways forward in your own classroom, department, school or cluster of schools so that, even if education cannot eradicate the 'Matthew effect', each person reading this book can, in his or her own way, weaken it.

The leaders who are the target audience are not just those with formally designated authority roles, such as head teachers/principals or deputies; rather, we understand leadership to be action based on values that is intended to influence the direction and outcomes in a school, or part of a school. Defined in this way, leadership is open to many, including teachers, learners and community members. Though leadership may be open to all, there is not equal access, as some groups are less likely to achieve a leadership role. For example, in many countries women teachers are less likely than men to progress to a leadership role. Teachers who are from minority ethnicity groups or from a minority religion or who have a disability are also less likely to become leaders. This is part of the inequality picture and we discuss it in Chapter 4.

The primary focus is on practice in schools in the countries of the UK, but we believe that much of the discussion will have relevance to those leading in Europe, in other parts of the world and in other education contexts. The first part of the book in Chapters 1 to 5 sets out some of the ideas and policies that form the context for those working towards greater equality in education. The chapters that follow focus on equality in relation to a number of areas: socioeconomic class, gender, sexuality, ethnicity, religion, migrant status and special leaning needs. Whilst the focus in each chapter is on a single characteristic, we include consideration of how other characteristics may interact with that characteristic to shape learning and outcomes. In Chapter 3 we consider this in more detail by exploring the idea of intersectionality.

We are dealing with complex ideas, each in a challenging and wide area of practice. Of necessity, this demands some selection, so we focus on the issues that schools may find most relevant or most challenging, or both. Each chapter will start with a brief summary of content and indicate the areas we would like you to think about. At the end of each chapter we summarize key action points, and include ideas about what it might be helpful to reflect on and discuss with colleagues, learners and the wider community. We also suggest further reading so that you can follow up areas that are particularly important to you. We hope that these elements at the end of each chapter will provide a useful basis for ongoing professional development focused on increasing equality.

Ideas of equality: so where do we start?

Most practitioners and policy makers in education would emphasize a commitment to equality as a fundamental value. The language may vary, referring not only to equality but also to related terms such as equity, social justice, inclusion and fairness. Each person, of course, will have a particular notion of what is implied by fairness, by equality and so on. However, often such understanding is quite hazy. It is uncommon for leader and teacher preparation programmes or for practitioners to engage explicitly with what is meant by equality and related terms.

Instead, we tend to use our experience as a means of understanding the context, to make assumptions and to decide how to respond. However, there are problems with this (Applebaum, 2008). First, our experience is shaped by our individual history and culture. Consequently, it may be a poor guide to understanding the experience of those who are very different from ourselves. Also, we tend to see ourselves as the hero of our own lives, so the way each of us may be part of an unjust system is obscured. We may discern unfairness in the way others act in other schools, but are less likely to recognize it in ourselves and in our own school, department or classroom.

For this reason, it is important that we each interrogate our commitment to equality and try to unpack what we mean by it, what the problem is and what we, together with others, can do to address it.

The justification for this book, therefore, and for the time you may give to reading it, is summed up in an aphorism from over two thousand years ago by the Roman historian, Livy: 'Experience is the teacher of fools'. This goes against a central belief in education: to progress in teaching or leading a school, it is assumed that experience counts for a great deal. Though there is initial teacher education and preparation for leadership roles, the major part of becoming a professional is through an apprenticeship model. We learn on the job from colleagues and from practising the art of teaching and leading. But what has been done before has led to the situation where schools offer a very unequal service to different groups. Chapter 4 outlines in more detail the evidence of how some groups of learners and staff are supported much more successfully than others. So learning by experience is likely merely to perpetuate a practice that has resulted in inequalities. In this sense, experience is an inadequate guide to challenging inequality.

A hard lesson for practitioners to accept is that they play some part in the production of inequality, and that what they have learned to date in their professional practice is unlikely to be adequate to change this. Better understanding of oneself and one's part in the current system is a foundation for setting out to challenge and change things, but it is a tough call. So the answer to the question, 'where do we start?' is in building our understanding of what goes on in education, how we are part of it, and how we might be clearer about our values and what needs to be done. This is the aim of the book.

Words and concepts

The way into exploring any area of practice is through language. The language in education is particularly tricky, being a minefield of related but different terms. 'Equity, equality, inequality, equal opportunity, affirmative action, social justice and, most recently, diversity' (Blackmore, 2009: 3) are in common use, each of which may be understood differently depending on organizational and national context. In the press of the everyday, we may assume that we know what we mean by a term and that others think the same, but this is unlikely. We need to consider how the language is used and link this to understanding the principles or criteria that each term generates, in order to make choices about policy and action; in effect, we need theory to underpin practice.

We make a start here by exploring four key concepts used widely – equality, equity, inclusion and social justice – to provoke thought about the practical implications of how they are understood and how inequality can be attacked in schools.

Equality

'Equality' is the term that is perhaps most widely used in education. In many contexts, equality is connected with sameness. For example, boys and girls are equal so they should be treated the same. The same tax should be levied on those with the same income. This kind of thinking is embedded in a much-quoted formula that is relevant to education:

> Assuming that there is a distribution of natural assets, those who are at the same level of talent and ability, and have the same willingness to use them should have the same prospects of success, regardless of their initial place in the social system. (Rawls, 1968: 73)

This seems a logical goal, but it falls apart quite quickly when related to education. The term used repeatedly, 'the same', is in the sense that two objects might be of the same weight or the same value. But children are not objects, and the 'talent and ability' and 'willingness' of each cannot be weighed against that of another to see if they are the same, because these very qualities in themselves may be shaped by unequal circumstance. Talent and motivation may not be absolute and innate, but forged by the conditions of upbringing and the experience of schooling.

In meritocratic societies such as that of the UK, people tend to see those who have more ability or make a greater effort as deserving a greater reward. A child who appears to have little ability in a specific subject, who does not try or is disruptive, may be judged less worthy of reward. Yet not only the child's background but also the experience of school may have led to such behaviour and so depressed potential ability. The curriculum and pedagogy may better support children with the kind of abilities and intended future path that mirror the experience of the majority of teachers. The 'Matthew effect' can be discerned in action. Those who are perceived to be talented and try harder, often from a background that has nurtured these qualities, thrive. Those who are perceived to have less, even if caused by circumstances beyond an individual's control, enter a downward spiral. Consequently, if equality is interpreted as expecting the same outcomes for those with similar abilities and effort, it is likely to favour those children who have experienced conditions that foster ability and motivation. Rawls' formula may not help much, in practice.

The 'sameness' Rawls refers to was a key component when equality legislation was established in Europe. Some believed that treating everybody the same embodies equality. Give the same curriculum to boys and girls – not domestic science for one and woodwork for the other. Ask the same questions of staff applying for a post – no probing family plans of women applicants only. However, whilst the examples given seem to offer equality, extending the idea to other areas soon raises problems. Is the same curriculum suitable for all? Can learners and staff with disabilities be treated the same as others? The same treatment may have a differential impact. Equality, therefore, is unlikely to be achieved by equal treatment, even of those who appear to have similar natural assets. Equal treatment is likely to reinforce existing inequalities: equal treatment offers unequal opportunities. A change in language from equal treatment to equal opportunities, the goal of much European policy and legislation in the 1960s, signalled a fundamental change in approach: that differences in treatment can achieve greater equality. The head teacher of Winburg School reflected on how this plays out in making provision suitable for every child:

Winburg: equal opportunities

I see it as about providing equal opportunities for everyone regardless of background, gender, sexuality or ethnicity. It is about equal opportunities in the curriculum, for outcomes and for accessing different parts of the school and making sure that provision is suited to everyone. The key thing is not to regard it as a bolt-on directed from the top, but something that suffuses the whole operation.

Equity

Equal opportunities is a widely used concept, as in the case example above, but for many it is an inadequate concept. Numerous organizations and individuals now use the term 'equity' instead, to indicate a different kind of intended outcome. Where equality relates to 'sameness', equity majors on 'difference', and indicates valuing different abilities and choices. Consequently, the aim cannot be the same outcomes for all. The Nobel Prize-winning economist Sen (2012) has been very influential in how we think about success in social organizations. He suggests we focus on a primary outcome of enabling people 'to lead the kind of lives they value – and have reason to value' (Sen, 1999: 18).

'Living a life they value' is a phrase that has resonated since. The goal here is different from equal opportunities. It is not so much based on statistical analysis of examination results, correlated with various individual characteristics such as ethnicity or socioeconomic background, or numbers going into higher education. Rather, it is ensuring that each individual is supported so that he or she feels they belong to school, enjoy it and develop the capabilities to live a life that is successful in their own terms and is positively embedded in society. This has come to be known as a capabilities approach.

Schools may assert that this is already a goal. The evidence however does not support this. Schools in the UK are generally structured and have systems that prize academic talents and trajectories. This may be due in part to national policies, as discussed in Chapter 2, but also relates to the practice of leaders and teachers. The relative value given to alternative vocational routes varies throughout Europe (Clarke and Winch, 2007; Hyland, 2002), but, generally, a hierarchy is evident in which the worth of particular choices reflects the culture of the more privileged. Not all children are equally supported to equip themselves to live a life they value (Hutton, 2005). For example, a recent review concluded that in Scotland an 'ingrained and frankly ill-informed culture that somehow vocational education is an inferior option' is prevalent (Commission for Developing Scotland's Young Workforce, 2014: 5). In England, West and Steedman (2003: 10) believe that vocational education is 'widely viewed as remedial'. The assertion that schools value difference, that they are equitable, seems doubtful.

As with the discussion of equality as a goal, equity too raises difficulties. A learner's choice to move outside family expectations and experience may have heavy costs emotionally (and financially). Encouraging all children who might, for example, go to university to consider doing so reflects a particular set of values that will be alien to some learners. Should they be supported to choose a 'kind of life they value' that is often based on their family background, even if they are capable of higher education? The tensions were captured well by the head teacher of Elands School:

Elands: careers guidance

I remember getting myself into trouble at a previous school because I was speaking to students after school and I was right in what I was saying, but the way I said it actually led to the cleaners in that block going on strike ... All I said was, 'If you don't get a good education you're going to end up doing a job like cleaning', which we know is highly likely, but it didn't make the cleaners feel particularly good about what they were doing.

The way we do it now is that we capture it in a slightly different way so when a student says, 'Well, I'm going to become a professional footballer so I don't have to worry about my education', we throw in little kinds of what I call disrupters, a bit of ambiguity. 'Of course that's great. The school will support you in that', but we say what happens if you tear a ligament and you are told you are never going to play again? What's the back-up plan? When a student says, 'I want to be a hairdresser like my mum', we say that's great, and if you got a degree from university you could be running a group of salons.

Whatever the interventions of a school, some learners will become cleaners or hairdressers or footballers. Staff attitudes to such outcomes need to be thought through. Does living a life of value inevitably involve higher education, skilled and more highly paid jobs? If so, it will inevitably exclude some.

Another difficulty is that throughout the world most policy that is aimed at achieving greater educational equity identifies groups who are perceived as disadvantaged and offers them additional attention or resources, or both; that is, improvement is aimed at selected groups, rather than considering the fitness of the system for all and improving it as a whole (Levin, 2003). One possible consequence of policy intended to improve equity, therefore, is that some groups of children are viewed as a problem to be solved, or that they and/or their family are in some way in deficit. As a consequence, many children not only suffer the effects of poverty, for example, but are then in effect also stigmatized, with the best of intentions in many cases, as a target for remediation.

To achieve a system that equips all 'to lead the kind of lives they value' (Sen, 1999: 18), the barrier or problem to be addressed is as much the school as the learner or the learner's family or community. This is one of the foundation messages throughout the book. We need to move the focus from fixing learners to fixing schools.

Inclusion

There is confusion in the UK about the term 'inclusion'. Ainscow (2005) charts its differing use over time from an aim to reduce truancy and exclusions, to the right of those with special needs to be educated in mainstream schools, to a broader understanding of accommodating difference and enabling participation. The broad understanding encompasses a need to remove barriers to learning and to achieve participation for all. For some, inclusion also involves feeling that you belong: to the school; to the community; to the nation. Ainscow suggests four key elements that define inclusion:

1. Inclusion is a process. That is to say, inclusion has to be seen as a never-ending search.
2. Inclusion is concerned with the identification and removal of barriers.
3. Inclusion is about the presence, participation and achievement of all students.
4. Inclusion involves a particular emphasis on those groups of learners who may be at risk of marginalization, exclusion or under-achievement. (adapted from Ainscow, 2005: 118–19)

This kind of comprehensive definition is less commonly used than that of the Organisation for Economic Co-operation and Development (OECD, 2012: 9). The OECD uses the term 'inclusion' specifically as an aspect of equity, which it defines as incorporating two elements: fairness and inclusion:

> Equity in education means that personal or social circumstances such as gender, ethnic origin or family background, are not obstacles to achieving educational potential (fairness) and that that all individuals reach at least a basic minimum level of skills (inclusion).

Consequently, inclusion is often used as the OECD does, to mean everybody achieving a basic level of education.

Consideration of what inclusion means leads to a further question: 'Inclusion into what?' Ainscow's definition suggests that it is not about helping struggling learners to adapt to the existing system, to be included in schools as they are, but transforming schools so that they are better matched to the needs and preferences of all and not just that portion of society that has been prioritized historically.

Social justice

Finally, there is the concept of social justice, embedded, for example, in the *Standards for Leadership and Management in Scotland* (GTCS, 2012). The concept of social justice is concerned with processes to reduce the kind of inequalities that education produces. Social justice as discussed by Furman (2012: 3) has a number of dimensions, all of which must be addressed together. First, 'distributive' justice demands that goods are shared out fairly. Goods here include emotional and intellectual, as well as physical, goods. So, for example, experienced teachers should be spread across schools in different socioeconomic contexts, across the ability range and not, as is often the case, just to 'good' schools, higher attainers or high-level courses. Second, 'cultural' justice demands action to address the domination of those groups that hold greater power in education, whether through socioeconomic advantage, such as the middle and upper classes, or by virtue of historically privileged characteristics such as gender or race. Racism and discrimination in relation to gender, sexuality or religion are targets here. Third, 'associational' justice aims to enable all to take a full part in decisions affecting their life, and to be critical and engaged learners and citizens.

This is a highly testing agenda for schools, but the central tenet is that all three – redistributing resources, ensuring all are equally included and empowering learners as critical citizens – need to be addressed simultaneously if social justice is to be achieved. The multi-dimensional approach generates an agenda for leaders' action in school:

> (a) They must raise the academic achievement of all the students in their school, that is, high test scores do matter; (b) they must prepare their students to live as critical citizens in society. (Capper et al., 2007: 111)

In short, social justice definitions demand that schools equip learners both to achieve in the current system and to challenge it. This is a second key message in the book.

So where to now?

The confusion around terminology is in part because equality, equity, inclusion and social justice overlap and are sometimes used interchangeably, as if they mean the same thing, and sometimes as if they mean different things. Having discussed the four most common terms used in relation to making schools fairer, the chapters that follow generally use 'equality' as a convenient generic term, signalling a focus on the kinds of issues discussed in this chapter. You may decide that another term is more appropriate for you, and we hope you are now better able to make the choice.

This chapter has argued that equal outcomes are not a practical goal in education. Rather, the aim is instead to focus on establishing a system in which all can feel they belong and achieve what is necessary to live a life they value. This implies treating learners and staff not the same but differently, compensating for previous disadvantage by distributing resources to favour those most in need, recognizing and valuing differing choices, rather than favouring, however inadvertently, the academic trajectory and White culture historically embedded in schools.

There is a film in which the hero wakes each morning to find it is the day before. The film title has generated an understanding of the phrase *Groundhog Day* (1993) to mean being caught in a never-ending cycle of the same happenings, only broken when fundamental change occurs in the individual. Schools are trapped in a 'Groundhog Day' where test results show that those from disadvantaged backgrounds or particular groups do less well than they should, and this finding appears again and again in reports from national and international organizations. If we are to break out of education's Groundhog Day, each leader and teacher needs to join with colleagues to make a transformative change in attitudes and practice to break the cycle. Not all will be on board. There may be conflict and failures. The default culture in schools is not fair, and leading change requires a clear vision and consistent, proactive action. In short, increasing equality in schools demands leadership from many.

Key actions

Changing understanding and attitudes is not easily captured by a neat, bulleted list in a way that might be easier for more focused areas of activity to increase equality. Nevertheless this chapter has suggested some key actions:

- Work with colleagues to identify the range of terms in use in your department or school: equality, equity, inclusion, fairness, diversity, social justice, etc.
- Identify the assumptions that underlie the terms used and the outcomes intended. What kind of sameness or difference is implied in how children are treated or what they achieve?
- Challenge thinking that sees learners or their families as being in deficit, and instead identify what it is in the school that may be a barrier to learning.
- Agree with colleagues and the wider community what your school or department would look like if it was equitable or socially just. What are the goals? What indicators might demonstrate this?

For reflection and discussion

In what ways does your organization or part of it embody the 'Matthew effect'? Consider the curriculum, pedagogy, use of resources and relationships with families and carers.

Additional reading

Ainscow, M. (2005) 'Developing inclusive education systems: what are the levers for change?', *Journal of Educational Change*, 6 (2): 109–24.

Levin, B. (2003) *Approaches to Equity in Policy for Lifelong Learning*. Paris: OECD. www.oxydiane.net/IMG/pdf/OECD_Eq_backgr.pdf (accessed 27.04.16).

Lumby, J. with Coleman, M. (2007) *Leadership and Diversity: Challenging Theory and Practice in Education*. London: Sage. Chapter 2, 'Equality approaches: what's in a name?', pp. 13–29.

Morrison, M. (2009) *Leadership and Learning: Matters of Social Justice*. Charlotte, NC: IAP.

Roemer, J.E. and Trannoy, A. (2013) *Equality of Opportunity*. http://cowles.yale.edu/sites/default/files/files/pub/d19/d1921.pdf (accessed 27.04.16).

Saito, M. (2003) 'Amartya Sen's capability approach to education: a critical exploration', *Journal of Philosophy of Education*, 37 (1): 17–33.

Walker, M. (2005) 'Amartya Sen's capability approach and education', *Educational Action Research*, 13 (1): 103–10.

For a more detailed explanation of the nature of types of school in the UK refer to www.gov.uk/types-of-school/overview (accessed 27.04.16).

2

The policy landscape

Education policy forms the framework within which schools act to increase equality. Practitioners want policy to be a support to their efforts and some believe it is working in this way. Others believe the contrary: that public policy is limiting or even working counter to their intentions. This chapter focuses on the policies in the UK and more widely to explore the policy landscape in which schools work. The overall aim of the chapter is to enable you to understand better the policy freedoms and restrictions within which school leaders and teachers aspire to promote greater equality.

> In this chapter we ask you to think about:
>
> - what we mean by public policy as it relates to education and equality
> - widespread policy approaches and effects relevant to equality
> - the response of educators.

Case examples to illustrate points are drawn from four schools: Revel Girls' Academy (11–18) in inner London; and, in the south of England, Darnall All-age Academy, Winburg Academy (11–18) and Allenridge Community School (11–18), all co-educational.

The tricky notion of policy

Policy can be set at a number of levels: classroom, department, school, region and nation. Our focus in this chapter is on the state level that we are calling public policy. In some parts of Europe, this is set at a national level.

In federated systems, regions may set policy. A simple, rational concept of public policy is that government agrees goals and the means to achieve them, sets these down in a text that becomes law, then schools implement what is intended. Rarely, if ever, is it so straightforward. More complex notions of policy suggest that interested parties consult, lobby and spin to influence a debate, which then shapes who is involved in the process, what policy is decided and to what purpose. The implementation may involve those who support the policy and those who resist it. The results may be those intended or some that are quite different, or both (Rizvi and Lingard, 2009). School leaders and teachers are at the centre of this messy process and, though they may not be able to avoid the impact of policy, they always have choices about how to respond.

Policies changing across Europe

Policy relevant to equality in education can be viewed from a number of perspectives:

- economic and employment policy, which impacts on the post-compulsory education, training and job prospects of young people
- social and family policy, which influences the personal circumstances within which each child grows up
- education policy, which shapes the schools that children have access to, and what and how they are taught and assessed.

All of these policy areas change frequently and are specific to context. Nevertheless, within the UK and more widely some trends are evident.

Economic and employment policy

Within Europe, economic policy is intended to increase participation in education and to improve training and employment prospects. Policy has not proved effective in many cases. In England in 2015, 13 per cent of 16–24 year olds were not in education, employment or training (NEET) (DfE, 2015b). Approximately three-quarters of a million or 16 per cent of economically active 16–24 year olds were unemployed in the first half of 2015 (Dar, 2015). Across Europe in the same period, youth unemployment rates were high, with the percentage varying widely between states. The lowest rate was Germany, at 7 per cent. The highest included Italy at 41 per cent, Croatia at 44 per cent, Spain at 49 per cent and Greece at 50 per cent (Eurostat, 2015).The percentages have dropped a little since 2013. Nevertheless, in countries with very high youth unemployment the bleak probable future for many children overshadows all other relevant policy aimed at improving equality in education. For many, the age-old bargain offered by education, that if children work hard and achieve they can anticipate a bright future, will no longer hold.

Social and family policy

Social and family policies have had little more success in supporting equality. Though poverty is defined in many different ways, there is nevertheless a clear picture that some groups suffer relatively greater poverty. One of these groups is children. Across Europe in 2011, 27 per cent of children were at risk of poverty; that is, their family's income was below the poverty threshold (European Union, 2015a). This average obscures a very wide range, from 13 per cent in Norway to 52 per cent in Bulgaria (Kern, 2015; López Vilaplana, 2013). Poverty does not mean the same thing throughout Europe, as the poverty threshold varies from country to country. For example, the UK threshold is about five times higher than that for Romania.

Amongst children as a whole are those in certain groups, such as Roma, who are particularly disadvantaged; 71 per cent of Roma families live in deep poverty and this is reflected in their ability to access education. The highest rate in Europe for graduation from secondary school by Roma children is 29 per cent, and in some countries it is much lower (Farkas, 2014).

The policies intended to reduce such poverty and to support children and families vary widely in their effectiveness. The European Union estimates that the most effective reduce the risk of poverty by 60 per cent and the least by less than 15 per cent (European Union, 2015a). The European Commission (2014) has established national targets for the reduction of poverty and early school leaving to be achieved by 2020. Whether they will be achieved remains to be seen, but meanwhile it is clear that many children grow up in circumstances that profoundly undermine their capacity for learning. As the case example of Revel School shows, shifting a mindset that has been formed by troubled circumstances, including but not restricted to poverty, is sometimes successful and sometimes not:

Revel: learners' self-belief

It's the not being in the right mind space to take up the opportunities that are in front of you and that often stems from having a troubled family. That would apply across ethnic groups and across class to some extent. It is where students are so caught up in life challenges that they are unable to grasp basic learning opportunities ... They have a stuck mindset after a challenging start to life. This mindset is often skewed to the poverty end of the spectrum, but not completely. It may be that parents have split up, are on drugs or have mental health issues and there is social services involvement. The child develops in a way that they are completely dependent on others and are unable to take responsibility or initiative for themselves and therefore can't access growth and development. We are a strong community. We inspire girls to aspire and do better but a few can't respond. They are unable to believe in themselves.

Economic and social policies may impact much more strongly on how far schools are able to offer equality than educational policies themselves. If children are hungry or constantly anxious or without security, learning is compromised. It is not only the emotional stress resulting from living in poverty that may distract learners. It is clear that cognitive development may also be impeded, so that the fundamental means to learn, the brain and personality, are altered (Lumby, 2015). Yet, as Jensen (2009) insists, some children in poverty do succeed, and schools can and do make a difference. Approaches to pastoral care and teaching, and learning pioneered in schools in communities of multiple deprivation, may be ever more widely relevant.

Education policy

Worldwide, education policy has developed to reflect twin principles: choice and competition (Henry, 2001). Choice is argued to be a democratic right and to have the additional advantage of driving up standards, as schools vie for pupils and reputation (Gibbons et al., 2008). Choice in effect implies competition, as in many parts of Europe schools can no longer assume that children will attend their local school or be allocated by a district or regional system. In many cases, staff must make efforts to maintain or increase the school intake.

This education policy shift has been proceeding for several decades. Ward et al. (2015) argue that Margaret Thatcher as Prime Minster in 1997 began 'the process of dismantling the welfare state in favour of the free market' (2015: 3) in England. One result of this policy in England and elsewhere has been the marketization and increasingly frequent privatization of education. Privatization involves importing values and practice from commercial organizations and, in some cases, giving control of schools to for-profit companies. The language or discourse used around this trend is rarely explicitly market or profit or corporate in nature. Rather, it uses 'terms of "choice", "accountability", "school improvement", "devolution", "contestability" or "effectiveness"' (2015: 8) and the associated values, policies and practice are evident across Europe and globally. The impact is felt in all aspects of schooling (Ball and Youdell, 2008).

The policy context changes not only what is done in schools, teaching and learning, but also the relationships between staff and children, between staff, and between staff and parents. The pressures of performativity, that is, constant scrutiny by means of league tables or inspection, accompanied by fear of potential public exposure, are particularly corrosive. Jeffrey (2002) suggests that relationships in primary schools have changed in three ways. In summary, the pressure of the performativity context:

- increases the distance between teachers and students
- makes relationships between staff more hierarchical, with less room for individuality
- makes teachers subject to inspectors rather than partners in development, as previously.

Hall and Noyes' (2009: 4) case study provides evidence of similar changes in a secondary school and of how it feels to teach within self-evaluation systems that are primarily intended to prevent negative inspection judgements:

> The pressures of lesson observation were intense, immediate and physical – Cathy described them as 'like a kick in the teeth' and Bill spoke of being beaten with a hammer – self-evaluation created its own kinds of pressures: more work, less time and a change in the sense of what the job of teaching was about.

The policy of choice and competition has put pressure on teachers' identities and practice.

Leadership is also modifying. Evidence is accumulating that policy changes have encouraged 'the kinds of leadership that seriously damage teachers, teaching, and student learning' (Blase and Blase, 2004: 245). Other accounts do not reflect such change where schools hang on to positive relationships as core to their work. This is the belief of the head teacher of Allenridge School:

Allenridge: relationships in the school community

Education is an organic process and relationships are all important ... being a friendly and affiliative organization is very important to us. We do not tolerate people being sarcastic, angry or petulant. We are a good-humoured adult community.

Not only relationships have come under pressure; in many cases, the curriculum and pedagogy have also been shaped by public policy, as experienced at Winburg School:

Winburg: policy narrows curriculum

One of the biggest threats to equality is the damage done by this government; the curriculum has narrowed so much. Vocational qualifications are not there anymore and this has meant the disenfranchising of a sector of the population as there are less aspects of the curriculum that they can access. There is a whole range of skills that we don't teach any more.

Overall, evidence of the negative effects of public policy in England suggests that equality for both staff and learners may have suffered. Those schools judged to be underperforming are subjected to intense pressure as a result of their perceived non-compliance with the new culture. For example, a teaching union officer interviewed for this book believed that a display of 'outwardly macho behaviours' is often a requirement by governors and parents, for head teachers and deputies to match their ideal of an effective leader, particularly in schools in contexts of multiple deprivation. This serves to disadvantage those who wish to lead in a different or more feminine style. Such perceptions may therefore prevent the application and appointment of talented and effective leaders who do not match predominant notions about strong leadership. Women are particularly disadvantaged (Lumby, 2015).

There is also an impact on equality for learners. In England, some schools are reluctant to accept children likely to bring down their league table position, such as those with special needs, as discussed in Chapter 12 (West and Hind, 2003). Schools may adopt a narrower curriculum, focusing on league table priorities (Wiggins and Tymms, 2002) and offer inadequate advice about post-compulsory options in order to discourage students, and the income they bring, from moving to another school or college (Foskett et al., 2008).

Relations with the wider community have also changed. The case example of Darnall School illustrates regret at the loss of support concerning Black and Minority Ethnic (BME) learners from the local authority (LA) as public policy removed its responsibility for school development:

Darnall: support networks dismantled

The local authority used to offer support to the schools through the Minority Ethnic Organisation. That gave us access to translators and consultants. Every school had an ethnic minority faculty that came under special educational needs. The county had a good support network and there was a Black and Minority Ethnic consultant assigned to each school. They offered support and things like free conferences and courses. That has all gone with the reduction in LA funding and supporting children with English as an additional language is now all up to the schools themselves.

However, she goes on to say, 'We do it really well in this school'. In the absence of support, she believes the school has learned to respond to learner needs itself.

Though there is much evidence suggesting negative effects of public policy, not everything points in this direction. Some school leaders have embraced public policy changes as bringing benefits, not least an opportunity to have greater control at school or federation level, as at Darnall School. Such schools feel that they sustain what is important in their practice. For example, in Hall and Noyes' (2009: 6) case study, a deputy head believed: 'Schools have changed tremendously but I don't think we've lost that very important thing which is the relationships between staff and children'. His belief is that what matters most, staff–pupil relationships, remains intact.

The evidence on how policy has influenced outcomes is complex and contradictory. For example, in England analysis of evidence suggests that those schools that have become academies have improved performance more than non-academy schools (Eyles and Machin, 2014). Other analysis of evidence suggests the opposite (Wrigley and Kalambouka, 2012). Larsen et al. (2011) consider the overall evidence and show some academies doing well and others not, just as one might expect with any kind of school. Whatever comparison of 'before and after' is undertaken to judge the success of a policy, the statistics can generally be manipulated to show more or less positive results. It is up to you to review the impact in your school of any policy area and, as a result of your analysis, to make adjustments to embrace the policy or mitigate it as far as possible.

Leaders' and teachers' response

Nearly fifty years ago Hirschman (1970) suggested that all human institutions are bound to fail to some extent, and each of us have three options in response: exit, voice or loyalty. Exit is leaving the organization. Voice is speaking up to try to change the things with which you disagree, and loyalty is supporting the organization. In schools, exit is a frequent choice in response, at least in part, to conditions brought about by policy. Though the exact percentage of teachers leaving teaching in the first five years is contested, it is clear it is high in many countries and may reach as much as 40 per cent (Schaefer, 2013). Learner exit is evident, at just over 4 per cent absence (DfE, 2015a). Loyalty is evident in those who thrive in the new system, for example head teachers who are credited with turning around failing schools, executive head teachers of academy chains and those learners whom the curriculum and assessment regime suits. Voice is evident in the trade unions that document increasing levels of stress and health issues, or the academics who adopt a critical analysis of the effects of policy. Learners who disrupt are using voice, albeit inexpertly.

Gleeson and Shain (1999: 474) focused on those who reject exit as an option, remain in the profession and must, therefore, accommodate public policy to some degree. They modelled three kinds of response of leaders to public policy: compliance that is 'willing, unwilling and strategic'. Willing compliers accept the rationale for using performance management and competition to better children's experience. Unwilling compliers are negative about public policy changes and direction: 'Anger and frustration with one's lot is discernible, across the age, gender, qualifications and range of experience' (Gleeson and Shain, 1999: 479). The majority are strategic compliers; that is, they find ways to reconcile their values with daily practice and to mitigate or circumvent those policy aspects that appear most unacceptable. It is not so much using active overt resistance, rather 'a form of artful pragmatism' (Gleeson and Shain, 1999: 482). Educators attempt to transform policy into something positive for the children they serve.

Public policy and equality

As outlined in Chapter 1, education is not performing well in reducing inequality. Schools in England, Germany and Scotland have all been highlighted as not serving the most vulnerable children adequately (Heineck and Riphahn, 2007; Sosu and Ellis, 2014). This is despite considerable public policy efforts to reduce inequality. For example, Scotland has embedded standards for social justice at every stage of an educator's career (GTCS, 2012). From those aspiring to become teachers to experienced leaders, all are encouraged to reflect on explicit values relating to equality and justice by reference to the standards. England introduced a 'pupil premium' as additional funding for schools with disadvantaged learners in a policy initiative to reduce inequality (Abbott et al., 2015; Macleod et al., 2015).

Though policy may be intended to make education fairer, it is often constrained by a wish not to disturb a system that advantages the middle and upper classes (Ball, 2003). Also, policy may be negated or overwhelmed by the power of vested interests and the status quo. For example, academies and free schools were conceived as a means of shifting power to teachers and parents so that they could establish and run schools offering better quality education, particularly to disadvantaged students. These policies have opened a door to for-profit companies, eager to enter the market of education (Miller, 2011). Though they must give thought to providing for their learners, profit is a fundamental concern, as in all corporations. Free schools are largely set up by middle-class parents who have the necessary financial resources and capabilities (Ball and Youdell, 2008). Intentions to increase equality are subverted, not so much by individuals intending to do so as by structures and systems that shape who holds power in education. Those who have historically been able to run education remain in control.

It is tempting for school leaders and teachers to blame public policy as the primary cause of the persistence of inequality, but they themselves also play a part. For example, choice policies may have exacerbated socioeconomic clustering (Agirdag et al., 2012; Croxford, 2001). Those who can afford to move into the catchment of a particular school have a genuine choice denied to those who cannot access such housing, leading to segregated schools with concentrations of middle-class or working-class children. Teachers reinforce such divisions when they aspire to a post in a 'good' school (Peske and Haycock, 2006). The latter are, in many cases, simply schools with an advantaged intake. The 'Matthew effect' referred to in Chapter 1 is seen when students who are advantaged cluster together and are more likely to be taught by experienced, successful teachers who can pick and choose their school.

Subject choice and career guidance are further areas where teachers' practice may not be in the best interests of all. Those who are passionately committed to their subject and wish for sustainable groups of able students to teach at a high level may inappropriately 'sell' their subject; they are amongst the willing compliers.

However, there are also many dedicated staff who choose to teach in schools in disadvantaged locations or with a highly diverse intake and whose wish, above all, is less related to their own preferences and interests than to the need to serve all children inclusively. These are likely to be the strategic compliers. Such leaders and teachers find ways to use public policy positively or to mitigate it.

Wriggle room

Ball (2006: 12) insists that:

> Policies do not normally tell you what to do; they create circumstances in which the range of options available in deciding what to do are narrowed or changed. A response must still be put together, constructed in context, offset against other expectations. All of this involves creative social action not robotic reactivity.

Whatever the public policy framework, educators retain choices. This is not to minimize or ignore the tensions, pressures and limitations created by public policy, but to suggest positively that educators always retain some power to shape the experience of learners, and doing so is their professional obligation and pride.

Key actions

It has been argued that many educators have become so accustomed to the discourse of public policy around choice, accountability, effectiveness and so on that they cannot imagine a different way of thinking. In responding to public policy, key actions may be more to do with developing an ability to unpack the language and ideas in use to better understand how policy is impacting on equality.

• Engage where possible to influence policy, through government consultations, teaching unions, subject associations and other relevant organizations.

- Identify those public policies intended to support learners from disadvantaged backgrounds or marginalized groups that are relevant to your school. Analyse how far they are increasing or decreasing inequality. Work with colleagues to adjust action, if necessary, to increase positive and mitigate any negative effects.
- Empower learners so they can influence policy in the short and longer term. Work to embed a curriculum of dissent that encourages students to develop skills of critical thinking and confident communication, so they can contribute to and challenge school and public policy.

For reflection and discussion

In what ways has public policy most impacted on the equality of learners' experience in your organization? Are these positive or negative or a mix? To what degree have you and other school members accepted or moderated their effects and to what end?

Additional reading

Ball, S.J. (1993) 'What is policy? Texts, trajectories and toolboxes', *Discourse: Studies in the Cultural Politics of Education*, 13 (2): 10–17.

Ball, S.J. (2009) 'Privatising education, privatising education policy, privatising educational research: network governance and the "competition state"', *Journal of Education Policy*, 24 (1): 83–99.

Field, S., Kuczera, M. and Pont, B. (2007) *No More Failures: Ten Steps to Equity in Education*, Summary and Policy Recommendations. Paris: OECD. www.oxydiane.net/IMG/pdf/No_More_Failure.pdf (accessed 27.04.16).

Foskett, N. and Lumby, J. (2003) *Leading and Managing Education: International Dimensions*. London: Paul Chapman.

Levin, B. (2003) *Approaches to Equity in Policy for Lifelong Learning*. Paris: OECD. www.oxydiane.net/IMG/pdf/OECD_Eq_backgr.pdf (accessed 27.04.16).

OECD (2012) *Equity and Quality in Education: Supporting Disadvantaged Students and Schools*. Paris: OECD. www.oecd.org/education/school/50293148.pdf (accessed 27.04.16).

Põder, K., Kerem, K. and Lauri, T. (2013) 'Efficiency and equity within European education systems and school choice policy: bridging qualitative and quantitative approaches', *Journal of School Choice*, 7 (1): 1–36.

Rizvi, F. and Lingard, B. (2009) *Globalizing Education Policy*. London: Routledge.

3

Responding to single or multiple characteristics: Intersectionality challenges

One of the dilemmas of leading for equality is whether to focus on a single characteristic, such as gender or ethnicity, or to consider the joint impact of multiple characteristics. A focus on a single characteristic might entail initiatives related to the needs, for example, of boys or gay young people. A focus on multiple characteristics, termed 'intersectionality', insists that nothing is so simple. Boys are not just male but from a particular socioeconomic background, ethnic heritage and so on, and all these characteristics together intersect to influence how others respond to them, shaping their opportunities to learn. There are strong advocates for each of these approaches. This chapter aims to explore the arguments from both perspectives.

In this chapter we ask you to think about:

- how the concept of intersectionality came about
- the implications for practice of focusing on just one or on multiple characteristics of individual learners
- the arguments for and against adopting an intersectionality approach
- the stance we have taken in this book.

Case examples to illustrate points are drawn from three schools: Trichard Community Infants (co-educational 5–7) and Revel Girls' Academy (11–18), both in inner London; and Maclear School (co-educational 11–16) in the south of England.

Can it be so simple?

Much research and guidance for practitioners related to equality focuses on the issues and challenges raised by learners who have a particular characteristic, such as their gender, ethnicity, special learning need, religion and so on. The performance of learners is generally monitored at school or national level by comparing groups with specific characteristics. For example, comparison is made between boys and girls, between ethnic groups, or between those on free school meals (FSM), a signifier of socioeconomic status (SES), and those who are not. Such an approach is termed by some 'essentialism'; that is, assuming that there is some commonality or essence that connects a group.

Dissatisfaction with this approach is long-standing. Black commentators have insisted for more than a century that the discrimination they encounter is a response not just to their ethnicity, but also to their gender, or socioeconomic class, or religion, or all of these factors (Du Bois, 1903/1968). Black women have objected to feminist writing that assumes the experience of all women is the same, and does not recognize how ethnicity and religion may interact with gender to shape their experience. Consequently, it is argued that research and writing about girls, for instance, is simplistic and misses an important understanding of how characteristics other than gender may also be crucial. For example, Ferri and Connor (2010) report a study of girls with special needs. They found that the girls' gender is significant in how others respond to them and it also influences reactions to their special needs. Often the only girl in their special educational needs (SEN) class, they attempt to retain credibility as a 'cool' girl whilst navigating the stigma of having special learning needs.

School leaders are well aware of this complexity. The head teacher of Trichard School explained that in her school there was great diversity in terms of the socioeconomic status of families, yet that many other differences also worked in concert:

Trichard: complex multiple communities in an infant school

There are different communities, for example there is a less well-off White British community, a well-off British/European community, a

Bengali community, a Somali community, and there are some families such as Congolese or Afghan who do not have a homogeneous community in that there is no one else who shares their language.

In this school socioeconomic status, ethnicity and language are all relevant factors to understanding the context in which children learn, and they do not neatly attach themselves to one per child or per group.

The concept of intersectionality

In recognition of this complexity, Crenshaw (1989) coined the term 'intersectionality'. Consideration of approaches to understanding and responding to the complex web of characteristics of individuals and groups has followed. The concept of intersectionality suggests more than a need to add together the effect of a number of characteristics like a mathematical sum. Rather, intersectionality implies that when an individual has two or more stigmatized characteristics, their experience is a distinctive result of the *interaction* of these factors.

The importance of the interaction of an individual's characteristics is illustrated in research undertaken in relation to people with disabilities. Stone and Colella (1996) found that people with disabilities generally encounter an initial automatic and largely negative response from others. This response is then modified by a number of other perceptions. Whether the person is perceived as physically attractive or the contrary makes a difference. Whether their disability is seen as the result of bad luck, such as accident or illness, or the result of their own choices, for example related to drug use or over-eating, also influences how people react. Even an individual's status makes a difference. A disabled individual of higher status is likely to receive a less negative response than an individual of lower status. Reactions to the disability of Baroness Grey-Thompson, the Olympic athlete, or the blind education minister, David Blunkett, are not likely to be similar to those to the disability of an unemployed person. Such research makes very clear how nuanced is the experience of an individual as a result of the interaction of multiple characteristics.

There are implications for practice. How far is it helpful to use the same approach to support a socioeconomically advantaged gay White young man and a socioeconomically disadvantaged gay White young woman? The experience of these two learners is probably worlds apart, yet they are likely to encounter some issues in common.

Intersectionality in schools

Staff are often aware of intersections of different characteristics as a highly complex web of different attitudes and needs amongst their learners and families. In the case example below, the head teacher of Revel School outlined how different factors impinge on the learning and progress of her students:

Revel: characteristics intersecting with gender

Intersectionality can be important. For example, if students have special needs, life's challenges are even more challenging. For young women that can be the case. In a girls' school it is confidence that is the real issue. As far as ethnicity is concerned ethnic minorities are dominant in the school body so that support from each other helps with confidence. A lot of the girls are religious and what I notice is that they accept what is said to them in relation to religion, whilst they are questioning in regard to everything else. Socioeconomic class is an issue as they have more of the initial challenges I was talking about earlier. They are not necessarily financially poorer, they may have the trainers and the TV, but culturally poorer in that they don't have a wider view of the world. Class is not defined as it used to be, but if you use those class terms, White working-class students are often particularly restricted in their mindset or in having lack of ambition or different ambitions, and who are we to judge? For example, the Traveller community are ambitious, but not in terms of a job and careers but in terms of marriage where they are very focused.

This head teacher reflects that an issue such as confidence building, relating to the gender of ethnic minority girls, is cross-cut by religion and special needs. Whereas learners can be supported to be confident to develop their own thinking in relation to much, in the area of religion this is not the case. She also refuses to treat those who are poor as a homogeneous group, and resists imposing middle-class ideas of aspiration on those who may have very different ambitions, such as Traveller communities.

Many of the staff we interviewed identified socioeconomic class as a key characteristic impacting on learning, but rarely was this unmoderated by additional characteristics. In particular, more and more schools have a highly ethnically diverse population. Sometimes minority ethnic students are viewed as constituting a single group, with English as an additional language (EAL) as the defining characteristic. However, practitioners in schools may experience this group of learners as anything but homogeneous. The feature that unites them, to develop English as an additional language, intersects with a wide range of other cultural, religious and socioeconomic factors, resulting in the complex mix of needs of each individual. Consider the perspective of staff in Maclear School:

Maclear: English as an additional language does not define an individual

Every Friday there's a list of students who are going to join us on the following Monday and always on the list there are students from overseas, so we're taking them every week … and it is an attractive school for anybody in any community, if they know something about the nature of our school, which at present is 52 per cent with EAL. That's increased hugely over the last six/seven years, so we've gone from a third to at least a half. Over 49 languages are spoken, literally from Arabic to Zulu. I've got (children from) Cameroon, China, Spain, Poland, Lithuania, Mexico, Portugal, France, Latvia, South Africa, Guinea, Egypt, Zimbabwe, Iraq, India, Indonesia, Saudi.

Just because they are EAL students doesn't mean they have not another learning need. They might have an SEN need or they might be a vulnerable student so we have to go on individual cases of students here.

This school is not in a metropolitan city, as you might assume. The frequent arrival of children with very diverse backgrounds and needs is an increasingly common one in the UK and across Europe, as discussed in more detail in Chapter 11. Schools, then, though they may not use the term 'intersectionality', are highly aware of the complex mix of characteristics and experience, where each moderates others, that influences the learning experience of each child.

Implications for practice

It is difficult to argue against intersectionality as a concept. The contrary perspective that separates the world into single characteristic groups can seem nonsensical. It can lead to policy and practice based on the needs of very large groups, such as girls or boys, and is an extremely blunt approach. It can also seem disrespectful to imagine that the same policy and practice are relevant, for example, to girls or boys from different socioeconomic backgrounds or with a different ethnic heritage or religion. However, how does intersectionality translate into practice? If we take the concept to its logical conclusion, then schools must treat every pupil as an individual with a unique mix of characteristics. In principle, this might be admirable. In practice, it is difficult to achieve.

Much research has focused on individualizing learning, particularly relating to the growing possibilities offered by computers and social media (Beach and Dovemark, 2009; McLoughlin and Lee, 2010). Many schools attempt a personalized curriculum and pedagogy. Revel School provides an illustration of how a highly detailed scrutiny of data about learning and social activity is used to identify individual learning needs:

Revel: meeting individual needs

We treat everyone as an individual and as well as helping them access learning we want to ensure that they are happy. This is so inherent in the school that it is hard to pick out anything that does not apply to equality. We just keep on with opportunities but notice who is not able to access them.

We have huge spreadsheets, databases of all students, what they study, their progress, what interventions they have had, which clubs they belong to, what successes they have had, whether they have special needs, if they get the pupil premium (additional state funding for each disadvantaged student). We look at the data in particular ways. An example might be to pick out all ethnic White girls by how many have done a sports club this term. If none, then we make this a focus.

I have a data person in charge. I have a deputy head in charge of achievement and they look at learning, a deputy head for behaviour and safety and they look at involvement, and a third deputy who looks at Year 7 because we think that patterns start there. Anyone can look at the data but we focus through these three groups.

This approach mixes a focus on the individual and a focus on small groups, such as White girls.

Evidence of what personalized learning looks like in practice suggests that some degree of compromise is evident, as in this case example, when provision is tailored to small groups as well as to individuals. How far schools can genuinely tailor learning to each learner is constrained by a range of factors, including curriculum demands and resource limitations such as staff time. Only a minority of students receive a truly personalized curriculum, for example, the minority of students who spend part of their time outside school, such as at a further education college or real work environment. Even here, it is usually a small group rather than an individual that experiences an alternative curriculum. One example of genuine individual tailoring we came across was attaching a 15-year-old pupil to the school caretaker for part of each week to learn practical skills and a work ethic, when all other attempts to engage this learner had failed.

In all these instances, personalized learning is interpreted in a fairly narrow sense as the acquisition of knowledge and skills (Hwang et al., 2008). Learning in its broader sense, incorporating all elements of experience designed to develop the whole person, tends to stay outside the equation. This is not always so, as the illustration from Revel School demonstrates. Its data look at who is joining sports clubs, for instance, and so the approach is clearly broader than just formal learning.

Considering just one discipline for a moment throws some of the issues of practice into sharp relief. Focusing on the subject of physical education, Flintoff et al. (2008) point out that, whilst differences in attitudes to and involvement in physical education are known to differ between boys and girls, the impact of other characteristics has been considered to a much lesser extent. The concern of practitioners and researchers about gender has relegated ethnicity to a less important factor, and disability hardly gets a look-in at all. The head teacher and curriculum director at Maclear School believed religion was also a relevant factor in girls' sport:

Maclear: intersectionality and sport

We're very clear about the girls having as many opportunities as possible, for example in sport, and that's been interesting because a lot of them are still wearing their veils and long skirts and things but it hasn't stopped them: football, netball, all the sports, swimming.

Even the thinking about gender and physical education is culturally driven and creates priorities that may not be justifiable in equality terms.

For example, why boys do not access traditionally feminized physical activity, such as yoga, has drawn far less attention than why girls do not take up traditionally male sports, such as football. Flintoff et al. (2008) argue that, in order to understand the experience of each individual in relation to physical education, practitioners need to engage with the whole individual. Just looking at groups such as girls or boys may expose the differences between these groups, yet risks missing the differences within each group. An intersectionality approach, then, can be useful in considering equality in each subject.

Rejecting intersectionality

Just as there are many who argue strongly that to increase equality we must consider the experience of the whole individual in all its complexity, others argue equally strongly that to do so risks weakening the fight against inequality. It is not so much that the concept of intersectionality is rejected; rather, it is judged unlikely to have a strong enough impact on inequality. It is argued that the similarity of discrimination and inequity experienced by some groups is of such importance that the group must remain the focus for action. For example, though the educational and life experiences of girls who are White or Black, economically advantaged or disadvantaged may be very different, all girls are likely to encounter the same kind of prejudice and barriers, for example in studying traditionally male subjects and being free from sexual harassment. There is also a possibility that taking the focus away from a particular issue such as gender or ethnicity may give support to the view that the particular battle has been won and need not be considered any more.

As a consequence, some argue that we should retain a focus on groups of learners who share a key characteristic, for example socioeconomic class (Reay, 2006), ethnicity (Shields, 2004), disability (Quick et al., 2003), sexuality (Renold, 2000) and religion (Shah, 2006). While there may be subgroups within each, the point is that the group as a whole suffers disadvantage and to counter that we must look at the nature of the experience of that group of learners, and find policies and practice in response.

How to act?

As always in considering inequality, there is no simple answer to how to act. The structure of this book, with chapters on single characteristics such as gender and religion, speaks of our conviction that it is necessary some-times to focus on just one area, the better to understand the implications of a particular characteristic. However, in each chapter we also explore differences within the experience of a specific group, for example not just girls, but Black, Asian heritage or Muslim girls. It is not an either/or but a focus on both single and multiple characteristics. Just as in the Revel School case example, the head teacher was aware of the need to raise confidence amongst girls generally, but also that there was a need to consider how the religion of girls impacted on confidence.

Awareness of such nuances is the first step to ensuring policies and development do not inappropriately homogenize groups. Equally, unthink-ing commitment to individualized experience for every learner may be no more than a party line to avoid more robust planning for what is pos-sible. As so often in matters of equality, finding the right balance is the way forward.

One of the aims of this chapter was to explain the stance that we have taken in this book. We have made it clear that an intersectionality approach is evident in the practice of our case example schools, though staff may not always use the term. Understanding the concept of intersectionality is important in all schools. Professional development is crucial to understand the complex experience of students who are disadvantaged by multiple characteristics. Equally, the fight against racism, for example, or the limiting perceptions of children with disabilities may demand initiatives designed to help one particular group with a specific characteristic. It is not one or the other, but using both as a twin strategy to increase equality.

Key actions

- Map the characteristics of learners within the school to understand bet-ter the major and intersecting characteristics that may be impacting on how groups are perceived and their needs met.
- Decide on the nature of data to be collected and reviewed to reach a fine-grained understanding of the progress of learners, not only in attainment, but also in emotional and social achievement.
- Sustain development for staff to help them engage with data and avoid assumptions that lump together groups that may contain important differences. For example, policies on sexuality may benefit from discus-sion of how the response from fellow pupils may differ for gay boys and gay girls.

For reflection and discussion

How far are the school's equality policies and practice based on the single characteristics embedded in legislation? Does this result in essentializing groups? Would learners benefit from a finer grained consideration of their needs and progress?

Additional reading

Bhopal, K. and Maylor, U. (2013) *Educational Inequalities: Difference and Diversity in Schools and Higher Education* (Vol. 102). London: Routledge.

Bhopal, K. and Preston, J. (eds) (2012) *Intersectionality and 'Race' in Education*. London: Routledge.

Ferri, B.A. and Connor, D.J. (2010) '"I was the special ed. girl": urban working-class young women of colour', *Gender and Education*, 22 (1): 105–21.

Gillborn, D. and Mirza, H. (2000) *Education Inequality. Mapping Race, Class and Gender: A Synthesis of Research Evidence*. London: Office for Standards in Education.

Shah, S. (2006) 'Leading multiethnic schools: a new understanding of Muslim youth identity', *Journal of Educational Management, Administration and Leadership*, Special Edition on Leadership and Diversity, 34 (2): 215–37.

Valentine, G. (2007) 'Theorizing and researching intersectionality: a challenge for feminist geography', *Professional Geographer*, 59 (1): 10–21.

4

The inequality landscape: Some differences matter more than others

However you cut the education statistics, in the UK and Europe and across OECD countries shocking inequalities leap out. The implications for individuals go far beyond getting a good job. For example, the OECD uses data from 15 countries to demonstrate that those with poorer education on average live six years less than their better educated peers (Mackenbach et al., 2015). Those who achieve less in education are more likely to face social and economic problems during a shorter lifespan.

This chapter looks at a range of data to map the inequality landscape. The statistical data used are those available up to 2015, but exploring the situation at the time of writing is intended to highlight issues and challenges that are likely to persist for schools and those they serve.

In this chapter we ask you to think about:

- how in/equality can be gauged
- inequalities in attainment
- inequalities in the experience of school
- the importance of national, regional and school-level differences
- inequalities amongst staff.

The chapters in Part II of the book deal with a particular aspect of inequality and provide more detailed information about each. In this chapter, the aim is to establish that inequality is universal and significant in education, and to consider some of the issues when leaders and teachers gauge in/equality within their own school and internationally.

Case examples to illustrate points are drawn from Winburg Academy (co-educational 11–18) in the south of England, and from an interview with a national adviser to a teaching union.

Assessing inequality

Much of the information used to assess the nature and degree of equality uses statistical data that compare the educational outcomes of one group with another. Examination results or progression to further training or employment is a common focus. These are the tables or graphs that repeatedly show correlations between a particular characteristic, such as ethnic or socioeconomic background, and lesser achievement compared to the average of the population as a whole or to a comparator group. For example, internationally data regularly appear on the poor results of boys compared to girls (Legewie and DiPrete, 2012) or, in Europe, the educational attainment and progression of Roma children (O'Nions, 2010). Comparative data on attainment and participation at different phases of education and training are used by governments to assess equality and through mechanisms such as league tables or the requirement to publish examination results, schools are obliged to focus on assessing progress towards equality in this way.

However, many school leaders and teachers resist such a narrow understanding. They may make use of comparative statistical data on attainment, but also believe that equality resides in a much wider range of outcomes, such as personal and spiritual development or the well-being of the child. They insist that the experience of school matters; not just the journey's end but also the nature of the journey. An unhappy experience of school is both unfair in the present and undermining in the long term, potentially depressing both personal and academic development (Copeland et al., 2013). The head teacher of Winburg School explained:

Winburg: prioritising equality issues

Equality issues will affect students throughout their life and it is nonsense if we don't give them due attention compared to pushing students through a course that will not impact on their life in the same way ... you can monitor anything to death. What is important is the impact which is not always measurable – it is about ethos and harmony, and you can sense it when you go round the school.

Equality is about more than examination results

The capabilities approach to equality, as discussed in the first chapter, adopts a very different perspective from a narrow emphasis on accredited outcomes (Sen, 2012). Sen argued that outcomes are always going to vary because individuals make their own choices about goals. The aim, then, is not equal outcomes but for all children to be supported so they are able to live a life that they value in the here-and-now; that is, while in school, as well as in the future (Robeyns, 2005).

In the remainder of this chapter we look at issues about unequal attainment, then go on to explore how school is experienced by children and how far this is fair. We consider the interaction of factors at national, regional, school and within-school levels, which coalesce to increase or decrease equality. Finally, we explore the inequality experienced by staff. The latter is a critical issue, not only because it is unacceptable for the adults concerned but also because it undermines children's progress. The unequal representation of particular groups amongst teachers and leaders robs children of role models who are, for example, Black or minority ethnic or women. It also presents children with a living demonstration of unequal chances that even teachers, to whom they may look up, do not overcome.

Unequal outcomes

The first chapter refers to a parable in the Bible, in the Gospel of Matthew, which tells the tale of servants given money by their master for safe-keeping whilst he travels abroad. One servant is given ten bags of gold and increases it substantially by investing it, whilst the servant given only one bag is so afraid of losing the little he has that he merely hides it and eventually, in disgust, the master takes even that away. The map of attainment in public examinations is a demonstration of this 'Matthew effect'; it is the story in action. Sociologists have tried to capture this idea through the concept of social capital. Capital is money available for investment. In a capitalist society, those who have capital to invest can generally use it to make more. Social capital is the knowledge, the know-how, the resources in a family and the wider networks to which that family has access. For example, middle-class families are much more likely to be able to afford extra-curricular classes, stimulating holidays and cultural outings. They also have access to the experience of university and professional occupations through a network of friends and colleagues. Just as financial capital can be used to secure advantage, so social capital is invested in privileged children's education and drives inequalities in attainment, progression and, ultimately, employment and health.

There is a multitude of statistics showing differences in educational outcome that cannot be explained by differences in talent and effort alone. At every level of education and in every country, children from impoverished socioeconomic backgrounds achieve less, on average, than those from privileged backgrounds who can draw on their family's social capital (Gamoran, 2001; Ross et al., 2012). The result is an attainment gap, where the examination results of those in high- and low-income groups are persistently further apart than can be explained by differences in ability alone.

Some argue that this has been the case historically and will remain so; that schools cannot do other than reproduce the current divisions in society (Ball, 2003; Fitz et al., 2005). However, differences in the degree of inequality by country, by region and by school suggest that this is not inevitable. Change is possible. For example, as a result of a concerted effort, known as the London Challenge, intended to address a considerable attainment gap in schools in London, the gap has reduced considerably. The scale of this reduction is such that the Fair Education Alliance (2014) concluded that if all primary schools performed as well as those in London, the attainment gap in England would be reduced by 65 per cent.

Socioeconomic background is only one of a number of factors correlated with lesser attainment than other groups. Understanding the landscape of inequality demands that we get to grips with the complex lives of children. An intersectionality perspective, as discussed in Chapter 3, insists that we consider a range of factors that interact to shape the educational experience and outcomes of each individual. Gender, socioeconomic background, ethnicity and other characteristics interact and influence the unique experience of each learner, so that statements about extremely large groups of children or young people who hold a single characteristic in common, such as their gender or ethnic background, often conceal as much as they reveal.

A good example of how simplistic interpretation of figures relating to large groups can be misleading is provided by gender. As Chapter 7 discusses more fully, attainment figures of boys and girls are widely interpreted internationally as good news for girls. This oversimplification misses the difficulties that are encountered by some groups of girls and boys more than others of the same gender. Headlines from attainment statistics that consider the impact of one or perhaps two individual characteristics tell us something, but they do not, as sometimes seems to be assumed, give us a definitive picture about the groups in question.

Is the answer, then, to construct ever more complex statistical sets that manipulate multiple factors in relation to groups? How are Bangladeshi girls on free school meals doing compared to African Caribbean boys who are not? And how will knowing this help policy makers and practitioners? As we argued in Chapter 3, schools need to collect fine-grained data and understand in detail the experience of their learners. However, there is a point where cutting the data evermore finely becomes unhelpful. Each nation, region, school or department must decide where this point is. The most fundamental issue that emerges is the necessity for acute sensitivity on the part of policy makers and practitioners to the unique nature of each learner's experience. It is using evidence in relation to neither just individuals nor just groups, but marshalling both with awareness of the value and limitations in each case.

The experience of school

Children have the right to grow up 'in an atmosphere of happiness, love and understanding' (United Nations General Assembly, 1989: 1), as established by the United Nation's *Convention on the Rights of the Child*. The argument is not that children should be uniformly happy at all times. A degree of stress is sometimes necessary to achieve what is worthwhile, and consistent happiness and enjoyment are not the lot of human beings. Rather, the directive makes explicit the belief that no child can develop fully if the environment is one that is frequently experienced as oppressive or unhappy. Consequently, to map the inequality landscape we need evidence not just about outcomes as an endpoint of education but also about what it feels like to spend the majority of your childhood in school: whether this is an equally positive experience for all.

Many children find school a fulfilling part of life that supports them to achieve outcomes that they value greatly. They enjoy learning and social contact with teachers and peers, and receive feedback that stamps their success (Lumby, 2011). There is a European table that indicates how successfully schools create a happy environment for children. England ranks towards the bottom of this particular league table (Children's Society, 2015). It is clear that some children find the experience of school at best unhappy and unsuccessful, and at worst destructive and disabling. Assessing the proportions involved is difficult, as they vary from school to school. A 2015 Children's Society report found that only 26 per cent of children 'totally' enjoy going to school, and 28 per cent agreed with 'only a little' or 'not at all'. It concludes that one in nine children are unhappy with school.

Of most concern are the disaffected learners who are truants, or who passively disengage and often fail to learn. They are also likely to become the 7.5 per cent of 16–18 year olds who are not in education, employment or training (NEET) (DfE, 2015b). Figures in each of the countries of the UK are not comparable as they are collected in different ways, but it is clear that a significant minority of learners in the UK end their experience of learning as soon as the law allows, even when they do not have a viable alternative route for their future.

Evidence from many schools reflects the experience of children who feel that they are often treated disrespectfully, that their needs are not judged to be as important as those of others and who consequently dislike school intensely. For example, in the words of a learner in England:

> I don't feel like I'm noticed, like I just feel like I am brushed aside and they just get on with the people who can do the lesson and they say them two can't do it and they'll just leave them. That's how I feel. (Lumby, 2012a: 273)

or in Scotland:

> Some teachers convey a sense that they don't like pupils and treat you as if you are not worth bothering about. (Hamill and Boyd, 2002: 114)

and

> The teacher told me to get on with the work. I couldn't do it but he just said I should be able to. He asked me questions and I didn't know the answer. I ended up swearing at him and he then threw me out and told me to go to the Pupil Support Base. (Hamill and Boyd, 2002: 114)

The last quotation demonstrates a cycle recognizable to all educators, where an inability to cope with the demands of learning spirals into aggression and exclusion. Overall, England does less well than other countries in maintaining good relations between teachers and children (Children's Society, 2015).

Of course, there are children and young people whose unhappiness has its primary roots outside the school, for example with family or mental health issues, but there is evidence that schools play a part and that disaffection and disengagement are not equally distributed throughout each school population. A survey of 45 secondary schools in England found that 'enjoyment is positively associated with students having a professional background, those not eligible for free school meals, speaking English as a first language, and being female' (Gorard et al., 2008: 7). In other words, not only is comparatively less attainment associated with particular groups, but also a negative experience of the years spent in school is related to characteristics such as gender, socioeconomic background, ethnicity and first language. It is also associated with sexuality (Hunt and Jensen, 2007) and religion (van Driel, 2004).

It is not surprising that school is a negative experience for the same groups that achieve comparatively low attainment, but the issue is not just the impact of the negative experience on outcomes. Making school positive for all also matters because of the potential long-term damage caused by an unhappy experience in childhood and adolescence.

A report from Scotland (Commission for Developing Scotland's Young Workforce, 2014: 20) includes contributions from many who believe 'that our education system has largely focused on 50% of the pupils i.e. those with academic aspirations'. This belief has become so much of a truism that its importance may register insufficiently. Policy and practice tend to put a sticking plaster over the problem rather than addressing what causes the hurt. The emphasis has been on helping the disaffected cope with the current system rather than changing the system to meet the needs of all children (Flecha, 2011; Osler and Starkey, 2005). Not only may the curriculum and pedagogy be designed to meet the requirements of a group perceived as the norm, but the general ethos also. For all the assertions about equality and diversity, and celebration of difference, the evidence discussed in the chapters in Part II suggests that being seen as different – by class, sexuality, special learning need or ethnicity – frequently puts children at a disadvantage and that schools are in reality often far from accommodating difference.

The minority who find school a difficult place may respond in inappropriate ways that reflect their limitations as a child or young person. Lumby (2012a) points out that in mature adult relationships difficulties are usually seen as caused by the behaviour of both parties. In schools, the problem of disruptive or withdrawn behaviour is viewed differently. Slee (2011) argues that 'naughty' children are pathologized, their behaviour seen as deviant and in need of correction, rather than, as is sometimes the case, an understandable response to feeling excluded, unvalued and treated unfairly. Put simply, the problem of children's antipathy and negative response to school is located with the child alone instead of also with the teacher(s) or the school. This is a foundational aspect of how inequality is sustained.

Mapping inequality must then take into account how children experience school, as well as what they take away from it in the hard currency of examination results. As the Children's Society (2015: 11) points out, 'If schools do not measure the wellbeing of their children, but do measure their intellectual development, the latter will always take precedence'. There are lessons here about data collection, but adjustments are also needed in attitudes. Acknowledging that the problem lies at least partly with schools and the behaviour of staff and peers, not just with a deficit of individual learners, is necessary to address inequality.

Staff experience of inequality

So far in this chapter, the focus has been on inequalities related to learners, but staff also experience inequality. Characteristics such as gender, ethnicity, sexuality, disability and religion can and do impact negatively on the appointment of teachers and leaders and their experience of school. The relative paucity of data about the demographic profile of teachers and school leaders means it is difficult to give a definitive picture of how far chances of appointment and progression are fair. The most extensive data relate to gender. Many countries note gender differences amongst the teaching profession and those appointed to leadership roles. For example, the OECD Teaching and Learning International Survey (TALIS) (OECD, 2013) found that while 68 per cent of teachers are female, only 49 per cent are principals as a cross-country average. The survey offers no figures on other kinds of characteristic such as ethnicity, religion or disability. Locating such data entails searching through national databases and academic research. Often, the data have not been collected.

Available evidence suggests that, just as learners in stigmatized groups often experience school less positively than others and have lower attainment, staff with similar characteristics experience discrimination and progress less swiftly or less far in their career. BME staff (Ogunbawo, 2012), and those who are gay (Lugg and Tooms, 2010), disabled (Valle et al., 2004) or Muslim (Shah and Shaikh, 2010), are more likely to experience negative responses from governors, parents, other staff and learners than those who are in the majority. Gender also relates to barriers for both men and women. Women are still under-represented as leaders of schools, while men face assumptions about their sexuality when they wish to enter the most highly feminized areas of education such as preschool or nursery (Mills et al., 2004; Mistry and Sood, 2015). A national adviser to a teaching union whom we interviewed explains her experience:

National adviser to a teaching union: gender and expectations of leaders

School structures have changed. There are now more academies than maintained schools and many of these are in MATs (Multi-Academy Trusts). That change plus the punitive Ofsted accountability system may have led to a perception that 'you've got to be tough to survive', or at least display outwardly macho behaviours. This has been accentuated by inaccurate, alarmist media reports on student behaviour in schools which, coupled with a misrepresentation of the Chief Inspector's former comments on the heroic qualities of school head teachers/principals, may have contributed to a view from both governors and school leaders themselves that men have the stronger presence and are better equipped than women for the role of head teacher, particularly in challenging schools. Even though this is simply untrue, women leaders have themselves assumed that governors are seeking to appoint a man and need a great deal of encouragement to apply for them now.

Stereotypes that assume lesser competence come into play in relation to women and to many other groups (Lumby with Coleman, 2007), so some staff have to work harder than others to prove their worth and progress in their career (Bush et al., 2006; Coleman, 2007; Fuller, 2013).

Inequality in the system

Data on inequalities suggest that policy and practice in each nation, region and school contribute to or reduce inequalities. The OECD has established indicators of equity that it defines as incorporating two elements, as discussed in Chapter 1:

> Equity in education means that personal or social circumstances such as gender, ethnic origin or family background, are not obstacles to achieving educational potential (fairness) and that that all individuals reach at least a basic minimum level of skills (inclusion). (OECD, 2012: 9)

Considering both fairness and inclusion allows the OECD to address fundamental questions about the degree of equality and social mobility within each country. On this basis it argues that, contrary to what many people believe, increasing equity in education does not impact negatively on overall attainment. It highlights a number of countries that achieve a higher level both of attainment and equity than many others, and the advantages that accrue to the economy and individual well-being as a result. The OECD Secretary-General is unequivocal: '... there doesn't have to be a trade-off between growth and equality. On the contrary, the opening up of opportunity can spur stronger economic performance and improve living standards across the board' (OECD, n.d.). Statistics across the globe on the equity of education systems suggest that demography is not necessarily destiny. The national system plays a part.

There are also regional differences within nations. In England, the Fair Education Alliance (2014) mapped the attainment of a range of outcomes by region. It is clear from this evidence that some regions of England are more effective than others in meeting the needs of learners in low-income communities. In London 44 per cent and in the North-East of England 45 per cent of learners in schools serving low-income communities achieve the attainment expected in primary schools or better. In the Midlands it is 16 per cent, and in Yorkshire and Humberside 18 per cent. The Alliance suggests a range of explanations as to why some regions should be so much more successful than others.

Finally, the equality achieved by each school differs considerably. Ainscow et al. (2012) examined research undertaken in England over twenty years and highlighted how the kind of expectations, the way classes are organized and taught, relations between staff and children within the school and with the community beyond, and policies in relation to students in stigmatized groups all contribute to the increase or decrease of equality. State-funded schools in the UK work within the legislative and policy structure of their home country, yet the deal for the learners in each school varies considerably. Drilling down even further, there is stable long-term evidence of the differential effectiveness of individual school departments and teachers (Campbell et al., 2003; Creemers et al., 2010). School leaders and teachers, especially those who scrutinize value-added data tracking the learning journey of each student, are acutely aware of differential effectiveness within and between schools.

The key point here is that differences in the experience of education and its outcomes do not result from characteristics of the individual learner and their family alone, or the socioeconomic context of where they live. The nation and region also impact on chances; what nations, regions and schools do is part of the inequality landscape, as much as individual learners. The starting point for action is an acknowledgement that inequality is endemic and sustained at all levels of the education system. To move on from this, policy makers and practitioners need to fine-tune and scrutinize data within what Ainscow et al. (2012) call the ecology of inequality, looking to understand how what happens in the school, the region and the nation is a help or hindrance in decreasing inequality. They are then in a position to formulate policy and support for practice with greater awareness of the landscape of inequality.

Key actions

Data collection is imperative in order to understand the landscape of inequality at school, regional and national levels. Comparative data on attainment are an essential part of the picture of in/equality and are generally collected systematically. Leaders and teachers also need to monitor in/equalities in how children experience the ethos of the school, so data collection on children's well-being is equally important.

- Decide on and implement monitoring, based on comparisons of attainment and indicators of well-being.
- Analyse data not only by large group but also quite finely, to understand the differences within particular groups.
- Monitor how staff experience the school and their career progression.
- Use data on the performance of regions and nations as a benchmark and to point up relative effectiveness compared to other regions of the nation, Europe and the world.

For reflection and discussion

If you were to map the inequality landscape for your local context, where would be the most significant inequalities: within your own school, between your school and others, or between your region and other regions? We have argued for a fine-tuned and fine-grained scrutiny of data. Are such data accessible by teachers in your school in a way that they can use meaningfully?

Additional reading

Banerjee, R., Weare, K. and Farr, W. (2014) 'Working with "Social and Emotional Aspects of Learning" (SEAL): associations with school ethos, pupil social experiences, attendance, and attainment', *British Educational Research Journal*, 40 (4): 718–42.

Downey, C. and Kelly, A. (2013) 'Professional attitudes to the use of data in England'. In K. Schildkamp, M.K. Lai and L. Earl L (eds), *Data-based Decision Making in Education*. Netherlands: Springer, pp. 69–89.

Fair Education Alliance (2014) *Will We Ever Have a Fair Education for All? The Fair Education Alliance Report Card 2014*. http://static1.squarespace.com/static/543e665de4b0fbb2b140b291/t/5481a731e4b0d2f5ad3b39fb/1417783096688/FEA+Report+Card+2014.pdf (accessed 28.08.15).

Kelly, A. and Downey, C. (2011) *Using Effectiveness Data for School Improvement: Developing and Utilising Metrics*. Abingdon: Routledge.

Ladson-Billings, G. (2006) 'From the achievement gap to the education debt: understanding achievement in US schools', *Educational Researcher*, 35 (7): 3–12.

Thapa, A., Cohen, J., Guffey, S. and Higgins-D'Alessandro, A. (2013) 'A review of school climate research', *Review of Educational Research*, 83 (3): 357–85.

5

Approaches to attacking inequality

Einstein famously defined insanity as doing the same thing yet expecting different results. If he is right, then we cannot solve equality problems by using the kind of thinking we have used so far. We need to think differently and persist in the face of the likely resistance. Those who are advantaged by the current system have a vested interest in opposing change. Leaders and teachers may be amongst these if, for example, they work in 'good' schools or prefer delivering an academic curriculum to compliant learners. However, in opposition to such resistance are very many committed and dedicated staff, determined to do what they can to make education fairer.

How to bring about change is the perennial quest. It is always easier to diagnose the barriers to equality than thinking through and implementing solutions. Finding ways forward is especially tricky, given that the policy context may limit the options available to leaders and teachers. The first part of this chapter briefly considers key aspects of the context that may inhibit change. The chapter then goes on to consider big picture approaches to tackling inequality and explores specific tactics.

In this chapter we ask you to think about:

- critical aspects of the context that impact on equality
- approaches to increasing equality
- in-school strategies to increase equality.

Case examples to illustrate points are drawn from the community schools Allenridge (11–18), Elands and Maclear (11–16), and Winburg Academy (11–18), all in the south of England; and Blackberry Church of England Primary (5–11), a voluntary-aided rural village school in the east of England. All these schools are co-educational.

Context matters

Across the UK and Europe, education policy varies considerably, however not all aspects of the policy context are equally important in terms of increasing equality. The degree to which the system segregates children is a particularly critical factor. The 'Matthew effect' referred to in Chapters 1 and 4, where advantaged learners gain more and disadvantaged learners fall further behind, is exacerbated in systems in which children are segregated according to their socioeconomic background or another factor related to privilege. Where there is choice, for example between private and state-funded schools, between schools located in areas of private and social housing, or between selective and comprehensive schools, those who have more financial and social capital are able to and will generally opt for a school with the greatest concentration of children from privileged backgrounds (Ball, 2003). Any policy chink that allows segregation is eagerly sought by many keen to gain advantage for their child.

As discussed in Chapter 2, the ideology of market choice evident in so much education policy since the 1980s has exacerbated segregation in many countries. For example, there is mounting evidence of increasing segregation related to school choice in Germany (Kristen, 2003), Holland (Denessen et al., 2005), Sweden (Bohlmark and Lindahl, 2007), and England and Wales (Croxford, 2001), amongst others. Consequently, school leaders and teachers do not start with a 'level playing field' for themselves or their students. Generally speaking, schools with a majority of children from privileged backgrounds attract further advantages such as talented staff and more resources than schools where disadvantaged learners are clustered.

Segregation is also evident within schools. Again, there is considerable evidence that what is variously referred to as streaming, tracking or setting – that is, dividing children into groups according to their perceived ability – further disadvantages those learners that start behind. Some may assume this practice only relates to post-primary education. This is not the case. Hallam and Parsons (2013) use the millennium cohort study of children in all four countries of the UK to show that, even at primary school level, nearly one in five children is streamed; that is, they are placed and remain in a single class on the basis of perceived attainment. Their analysis shows that a number of factors other than attainment, such as behaviour and ethnicity, contribute to allocation to the top or bottom stream. They argue that streaming was rare from the late 1970s to 1990, and that a combination of successive governments' guidelines and teachers' response to the pressure to raise standards has led to an increase in its use, despite evidence that it exacerbates disadvantage.

The curriculum and the assessment system also form a restrictive framework. In Chapter 2, the head teacher of Winburg School suggested that government policy had restricted the curriculum to such an extent that the school could not meet the needs of all their learners. This leader placed responsibility with national government, but practitioners in schools also bear some responsibility for how the curriculum has evolved. Vocational qualifications have never been strong in UK schools, given the difficulty of recruiting teachers with a vocational background, and the reluctance of the majority of teachers to value and focus on this aspect of the curriculum.

Overall, national policies that increase or decrease segregation between and within schools and decisions about the nature of the curriculum and assessment inevitably create a context that limits what is possible. Nevertheless, as in the case of streaming in primary schools, leaders and teachers retain some choice and in themselves can strengthen or weaken structures and processes that relate to equality in schools. Leaders, teachers and learners can do much that will sustain current inequalities or begin to dismantle them.

Approaches to increasing equality

There is a range of approaches to adjusting a school to make both the process and outcomes more equitable. It is not possible or desirable to remove the advantaged background enjoyed by some learners at the starting point and throughout their education, but approaches to increasing equality are about trying to rebalance chances. Any number of metaphors might express this intention. For example, take the 'level playing field' – could this be 'tipped' to be more level? How soon after the starting point can this be affected? In the UK, the Sure Start programme attempted to provide a supportive preschool learning environment alongside childcare and parent education in order to address inequalities from a very early age. Intervention programmes such as nurture groups also try to rebalance chances early in the school experience. At whatever age it is directed in the learner age spectrum, all education provision can contribute to a rebalancing process.

Over time, three major strategies have emerged from research and practice:

- distributive justice through the redistribution of goods, including social as well as physical goods
- a recognition (Fraser, 1997) or cultural approach (Gewirtz and Cribb, 2002) through which marginalized groups are more strongly acknowledged and supported
- relational or participatory justice, where people are empowered to take a full part in relationships and in society (Lumby, 2013: 20).

Distributive justice

The first approach recalls Robin Hood. The riches in the system are reorganized so that they help those who are poorer. Some argue that this can be achieved with no negative impact on the advantaged, for example, by giving some learners more teacher time after school and so not at the expense of other learners. Mentors are another example of purely additional support, as they work with children perceived to be struggling and, in doing so, take nothing from those who are doing well.

Others argue that this interpretation simply dodges the point of redistribution. When resources are limited, as they inevitably are, increasing resource use in one part of the system depletes what is available overall. Redistribution of resources is therefore likely to trigger objections, resistance and a backlash from those who perceive themselves to be treated unfairly by the process. A cross-European survey of what learners consider to be fair found that the majority of learners in secondary schools in Belgium, Spain, France, Italy and the UK believe, for a school to be fair, teachers must give the same attention to all pupils (Gorard, 2012). The percentage that believed a fair school gave most attention to the least able varied widely from 46 per cent in Italy to only 13 per cent in the UK. Not only learners but also parents and staff may object to additional help being given to those, as they see it, whose ability, effort or behaviour do not merit it (Gorard et al., 2008).

Henry (2001: 29) assesses distributive justice as a weak approach as it essentially leaves the existing system untouched. An example is the additional resources sometimes directed to supporting girls to consider stereotypically male subjects, such as engineering or physics, because this sees the problem as being about girls' attitudes rather than the masculine culture within these disciplines. Counselling facilities for those subject to bullying or other negative reactions from their peers is another example of 'shoring up' a system that is unsatisfactory. Many might agree that this approach, which attempts to rectify deficits in learners or their families, has both value and distinct weaknesses.

Recognition or cultural approach

The recognition or cultural approach adopts a different stance. The problem here is not seen as the nature of any particular individual or group, but how they are perceived and treated. The intention is to acknowledge that the deficit lies with others, and aims to change their attitudes and actions to be more inclusive. Put simply, you do not have to be the same as the perceived norm to be valued. In some ways, then, this is the opposite of a redistribution approach where, instead of the individual being changed in order to achieve in the world 'as is', the community must change and adapt to accommodate better the many differences between learners. Implied is a differently structured education system, a different kind of curriculum and more inclusive pedagogies. A related notion is mainstreaming, where action to bring about greater equality is not merely discrete initiatives in relation to target groups, but rather changing the experience of all learners (Henry, 2001).

Relational or participatory justice

The third approach, relational or participatory justice, starts from the belief that change in societies and in schools is unlikely to be achieved consistently or quickly. This being the case, learners must be equipped to take a social and economic place in our existing unequal society, yet also be prepared to challenge and continue the fight to bring about change. All learners must reach a minimum threshold of achievement, however this alone is insufficient. Stitzlein (2012) argues strongly for the additional necessity to equip learners to dissent: to become dissenting citizens.

Flecha (2011: 8) recounts a transformation in schools in Spain in a community of multiple deprivation that welcomed a large number of migrant children in the face of much hostility to the incomers:

> It educated its students in both a *curriculum of access* and a *curriculum of dissent*, preparing children and youth to critically analyse inequalities in society. Meanwhile, it gave them the tools both to transform injustice and to gain access to socioeconomic benefits.

This approach does not exclude simultaneously working through distributive and recognition justice. A key point is that it is rarely one approach or another, but instead more than one at a time. Each of the three approaches on its own is partial and weak, while all three combined may go some distance towards achieving a powerful answer to the question of how to move forward.

Strategies in action: distributive justice

Redistributing resources, the Robin Hood approach, is most critical in the area of staffing, but is difficult to achieve. Schools that have an advantaged intake and are located in privileged communities find it easier to recruit talented and experienced teachers (Willms, 2006). Retaining such teachers is sometimes seen to involve allocating them to classes that can reach higher levels of attainment at an advanced level of study. Consequently, classes of children requiring a great deal of support to reach lower levels of attainment, or areas of study that are not academic, may not be attractive to teachers whose experience or talents give them the power to choose their post and whether they stay. A national US report is unequivocal: 'The very children who most need strong teachers are assigned, on average, to teachers with less experience, less education and less skill than those who teach other children' (Peske and Haycock, 2006: 2). Learners from minority groups or from low-income communities are more likely to be assigned to less experienced teachers and teachers who are not specialists in the subject being taught. The US report emphasizes that there are dedicated teachers who commit themselves to supporting learners from low-income communities or from minority groups, but it makes clear that these are the exception.

The situation is the same in England: 'there are problems with teacher recruitment and retention in deprived areas – teachers tend to be younger and turnover higher' (Prime Minister's Strategy Unit, 2005: 56). In 2014, the Chief Inspector of Schools for England warned that a shortage of teachers was exacerbating a situation where some schools 'cherry pick' the best trainees and teachers, risking 'a polarised education system where good schools get better at the expense of weaker schools' (Ofsted, 2014a: 22).

Three possible tactics are evident in response to the situation. First, though many teachers may be reluctant to teach in schools in low-income communities, it is nevertheless possible to insist on recruiting only those dedicated to meeting the challenge, as is demonstrated in Elands School:

Elands: recruiting appropriate staff

We're very adamant. I think this is like a key rule for the school, that when we interview new staff, new teachers, we get them to deliver a lesson and we expect it to be at least good and possibly outstanding and we won't appoint if we're short in that area and we won't take someone otherwise. We think our students deserve the very best. Ultimately, if you can recruit and retain the very best staff, the majority of what happens in the school will continue to move forward. Since we have followed that policy, the number of students that have been excluded has fallen and the number of students entering the school has increased by over 3 per cent, so you've got some clear evidence that the curriculum is now meeting the needs and aspirations of all the learners who use the school.

As well as recruiting committed staff, it may also be about removing staff who are not dedicated to increasing equality. In Maclear School the head teacher and curriculum director explained that it had taken many years to achieve an appropriate profile of teachers:

Maclear: inappropriate staff move on

We've got a very different staff team from the one we had when I came in seven and a half years ago, so people who haven't been prepared to work hard, really work to differentiate and meet the needs of a large variety of students in classrooms, have moved on. It hasn't suited them and we have moved quite a lot of them. I think that is key actually.

Additionally, avoidance as far as possible of streaming/setting within each school would remove classes where those from disadvantaged backgrounds cluster. Where some degree of streaming or setting is unavoidable, staff can be allocated so that the children who need most help to reach a basic threshold of education have their fair share of experienced teachers.

Ensuring all have fair access to experienced staff is an example of shifting physical resources that people can see and, therefore, easily understand. It may not be the only kind of resource that needs to be adjusted. Many learners find the distribution of power within schools, with staff holding much power and learners very little, provokes a sense of injustice to such a degree that it undermines their learning. Learners may gain approval and consequently power by being like most teachers, enjoying academic study and holding middle-class values. Learners who are not like this can be powerless. Learners' disengagement is often primarily due to this sense of powerlessness to challenge what they see as unfairness in the school system. They feel unvalued and given less attention than more high-attaining learners, and that their way of life and aspirations are judged inferior to the usual middle-class trajectory. Children and young people are not equipped to argue this case and the aggression or disruption that they sometimes substitute for reasoned discussion exacerbates the situation (Lumby, 2012a; Slee, 2014). Some schools have recognized this barrier to learning, particularly to those who feel marginalized in school, and have attempted to redistribute the more nebulous resource of power. An illustration comes from Elands School:

Elands: redistributing power through adjusting relative status

This leads us on to the role of our staffroom. We've got a shortage of space in the school and we had an SMT [senior management team] working day and we looked at the staffroom. So what we're going to do is a bit out there but I think it's a really good idea. I said whatever we do in the staffroom we can't be seen to be spending money on staff and not the students. So we're going to redesign it. We going to have a 1990s' bedroom-type poster element down one end with a pinball machine, arcade game and pool table. Down the other end we're going to have it like a New York skyline with sofas. The other side we're going to have it like a beach, palm trees, sandy beaches, beanbags and it's going to be a multi-use space. So not only does it become highly creative for the staff in the school, but ... also we are going to open it up to the students as well and are going to call it the VIP hub. So as a good example, on a student's birthday they'd get a VIP pass to take three friends to go up there for registration for 20 minutes in the morning. So it becomes their area, so we don't continue to have this divide; that's the staffroom and only the staff can go in there and no students because actually the staff don't go in there at all. It's a dead space during the day so we will make it a bit more creative and I think we can hit more students that way.

This tactic both redistributes physical space, making an area available to learners that is generally little used during the day, and also shifts the power relationship. A staffroom is a symbol of the status of staff; opening it up to students, particularly in a way that relates to youth culture and challenges notions of an academic quiet space, is a serious shift – a redistribution of both space and power.

Some schools have attempted a similar power shift by enrolling learners in off-site organizations that offer an alternative culture based on more equal power relations, for example a real work environment or a further education college. Evaluation of such work has tended to focus on the differences in the curriculum, but research suggests what is most valued and supportive of a renewed engagement with learning is a different power relationship between adults and learners. Here is the perception of a 15-year-old who struggled very much at school and was enrolled for two days a week at a further education college:

> It is better for people who have difficulties at school and most people have difficulties at school. More people don't like school than like school. College is more enjoyable than school. Mainly it's the freedom you get. It's a lot, lot better. You don't feel like everybody is constantly in your face and you have got no freedom and there are too many boundaries. At college you can always have time out from class. There are quite a lot of breaks. There are a lot of liberties you are given. It's a lot easier. There is less pressure. (Lumby, 2007: 6)

This learner assumes that most people feel as he does. This may not be the case but, as discussed in Chapter 4, a significant minority of learners do find the environment of school one where it is difficult to learn. The tactic used by the school relocates the learner to another culture where power is distributed differently. A few schools have created a discrete environment within the school itself, as a kind of haven where power relations differ, for example in a vocational training unit.

There are many resources that may benefit from redistribution to underpin efforts to increase equality. Staffing and power are just two examples. As argued earlier in this chapter, efforts are likely to be unsuccessful unless there are multiple approaches in play simultaneously, leading us to consider other approaches.

Strategies in action: a recognition or cultural approach

The chapters in this volume dealing, for example, with migrant children, issues of sexuality or ethnicity provide ample evidence that there are many groups that, even when resources are redistributed to support them, nevertheless remain perceived as outside a norm. In an environment such as Maclear School, where many languages are spoken and many cultures come together, the issue of mutual respect is high on the agenda. Also, a White middle-class norm is not so evident. For the many schools where children are all or mostly White and English is the home language of the majority, it may take greater efforts by staff to recognize the need to embed diversity in all aspects of the curriculum and staffing. Consequently, a recognition approach is more challenging. In the case example of Blackberry School, the head teacher reflected that they have no same-sex parent families and no Black and ethnic minority learners, which means that a kind of reality in which to anchor values concerning diversity is absent. Neither were there any children with visible special learning needs until a child with Down's Syndrome arrived:

Blackberry: staff fears

My experience is across several schools and is broadly not the picture now in this school. Sometimes adults who work in schools can be a little 'sheltered' in their own experience and afraid of things that are a bit different. For example, where a child with Down's Syndrome joined the school, there was initially some resistance, as staff worried whether we could offer the right kind of learning environment. However, it quickly became apparent to all staff that a child with learning disabilities brings as much to a setting and to the richness of experience for children as that child derives from attending a setting.

The popular press sometimes promote the notion that schools with diverse learners face especially challenging problems. The case example of Blackberry School suggests that the opposite may be the case: that providing children with an appropriate education to thrive in twenty-first-century society is particularly difficult in settings where diversity is less apparent.

Many of the chapters in this book focus on tactics to ensure the needs of particular groups are recognized. This goes well beyond add-on 'celebrating diversity' events. It involves looking more critically and deeply at how the needs of specific groups are met in teaching and learning, and in the general environment. Chapter 9 discusses, for example, how learners with an ethnic minority heritage require a curriculum that reflects that heritage, a general school environment that fits their cultural preferences, and to see their heritage reflected in their teachers and leaders. An all-White staff may not necessarily be identified as an issue, because it is so often viewed as the unproblematic norm (Lumby and Heystek, 2012). The head teacher of Allenridge School did not see things this way and had made efforts to increase diversity amongst not just teachers but also the leadership of the school:

Allenridge: professional development for BME staff

We have created a course to be proactive about redressing the current BME staffing imbalance across the town, especially in senior leadership. If you were to attend meetings, it would be very apparent that there was only one head who was BME out of a very large number. The group feels very White, but in the urban area, in the 0–4 age group, 51 per cent of the children are BME and we need to be awake to that. We needed to create a course or programme to encourage minority ethnic people to aspire to leadership.

Adjusting staffing and the curriculum to recognize diversity may be diffi-cult. Nevertheless, just as the Glentanna School case example in Chapter 8 ensures that the literature the children read challenges heterosexual norms, so every aspect of the curriculum is open to adjustment away from narrow norms that reflect only a proportion of the population. Similarly, the exam-ples above show there are ways to recognize our diverse society in staffing if there is sufficient determination.

Strategies in action: relational or participatory justice

We have argued that an essential component for increasing equality is both to equip students to succeed in the circumstances that prevail and to develop critical thinking to enable them to challenge those circumstances. Hatcher (2006) points out that, ironically, it is academically high-attaining students who tend to have the most opportunity to develop critical think-ing, whilst disadvantaged students, who most need to change society, tend to experience learning as information processing and retention.

Furman and Shields (2005) provide a detailed agenda for constructing a 'curriculum of access and a curriculum of dissent' (Flecha, 2011: 8). The series of questions they ask provide a useful practical means for the school community to debate how things might need to change. For example, in terms of pedagogy, Furman and Shields (2005: 136) ask:

> Curriculum: What formal curriculum is in place and what perspectives does it represent? Who selected it? On what basis?
>
> Informal curriculum: What are the assumed norms, beliefs or values taught throughout the school? How are these communicated? Who is represented and who excluded by this conception of curriculum?
>
> Assessment: What are the dominant images of success and how are they assessed and legitimated?

However, those attempting to respond to such questions repeatedly encounter two barriers: equality or justice is seen as peripheral to the mainstream curriculum; and spending classroom time on equality issues is seen as unfair. It is argued to be unfair to the advantaged, who do not need the curriculum to change. It is also argued to be unfair to disadvantaged students, who need to spend all their time and effort on succeeding in the current system. 'Lessons and activities specifically designed to help students consider some causes of, and solutions for, persistent social, economic, and political inequities' (Shields and Mohan, 2008: 291) are criticized as 'a frivolous waste of precious school hours, especially for poor children, who start out with a disadvantage' (2008: 294). Despite this criticism, Shields and Mohan (2008: 297) argue strongly that the curriculum and pedagogy need to change fundamentally to what they call a 'curriculum as conversation', where:

> the goal for educators is to help students understand that all information presented as formal curriculum comes from a particular standpoint or bias. Thus, teaching students to ask about other perspectives, and to question, reflect, critique, and challenge, is a way to enhance understanding and the learning of content. This approach is, of course, very different from one that simply asks students to recall data presented to them and to provide appropriate pre-selected responses to test questions.

Besides the arguments that such teaching is peripheral and time wasting, many practitioners no doubt might add that it is also impractical within the current tight curriculum and assessment restrictions. It is for each practitioner to consider how far this is a legitimate objection and how far it is justification for retaining an approach to teaching that is familiar. In the case example of Winburg School, below, time is given to specifically develop skills to understand and critique society:

Winburg: embedding critical thinking

It is also about giving enough time for PSHE [personal, social and health education], which we call Values and Ethics here. You need time to debate equality issues and barriers and how society views people. We make sure there is enough time for this for the student body to debate and make sure that people realize the importance of equality in school.

Arguments that current pressures do not allow any flexibility in the curriculum sound hollow in the face of a determination such as this; there is time and space for anything considered of sufficiently high priority.

So where are we up to?

In this chapter we have considered three major approaches to achieving greater equality in schools in the light of the deep inequalities explored in Chapter 4. The approaches are linked to the ideas of equality and fairness explored in the first chapter, acknowledge the policy context explored in Chapter 2 and take into account intersectionality, as discussed in Chapter 3. No doubt the ideas we have presented have raised more questions than provided answers. The aim is to stimulate you to think about practice in your own classroom, department, school and network, and to find your own tailored ways forward.

Key actions

- Analyse the degree to which segregation by socioeconomic class or other characteristics is present in the school. Attempt to reduce or eliminate segregation.
- Monitor the use of experienced and less experienced staff, ensuring that the most senior and experienced staff teach those most in need of effective support.
- Use the Furman and Shields' (2005) framework, or any other that seems to you appropriate, to interrogate curriculum and pedagogy and, as far as possible, embed recognition of multiple perspectives rather than primarily a single norm.

- Identify power relationships between staff and learners, and evaluate the degree to which they support learning. Adjust, if necessary, by shifting carriers of power such as space, access to resources, influence over the curriculum and pedagogy. Work to enhance a genuine student voice.
- Embed the development of critical skills and a critical perspective on society in the curriculum and pedagogy, so that all students are enabled to critique and respond to issues in society.

The chapters that follow take a more focused look at specific aspects of inequality and present in more detail some of the practice that we have come across in our case example schools. We hope the foundation of concepts and theories that we have presented in the first five chapters provides a good basis for you to move onward and learn more that can help you.

For reflection and discussion

Are you aware of the three approaches we have discussed in action in your school? Is there a preference for one approach more than another? Case examples tend to suggest that the third approach, equipping people to be critical thinkers and dissenting citizens, is the least common. Is this the case in your school and, if so, why?

Additional reading

Furman, G. and Shields, C. (2005) 'How can educational leaders promote and support social justice and democratic community in schools?', in W.A. Firestone and C. Riehl (eds), *A New Agenda for Research in Educational Leadership*. New York: Teachers College Press, pp. 119–37.

Hatcher, R. (2006) 'Social class and schooling: differentiation or democracy?', in M. Cole (ed.), *Education, Equality and Human Rights: Issues of Gender, Race, Sexuality, Disability and Social Class*. London: Routledge, pp. 202–24.

Lingard, B. and Mills. M. (2007) 'Pedagogies making a difference: issues of social justice and inclusion', *International Journal of Inclusive Education*, 11 (3): 233–44.

Smith, E. and Gorard, S. (2006) 'Pupils' views on equity in schools', *Compare: A Journal of Comparative and International Education*, 36 (1): 41–56.

Part II

Addressing in/equality

6

Socioeconomic class and equality

'Poverty is like punishment for a crime you didn't commit', the twentieth century writer Eli Khamarov famously said. It certainly works that way for millions of schoolchildren. Statistics presented throughout this book demonstrate that poverty overshadows or exacerbates all other factors in terms of a negative impact on learners. In England 'more than three out of five children from disadvantaged backgrounds leave school without achieving the basics of English and maths' (Fair Education Alliance, 2014: 1). In all countries of the European Union learners from low socioeconomic backgrounds perform worse than those from richer backgrounds, and across OECD countries such learners are twice as likely to be low attainers than their wealthier peers (OECD, 2012). Although this outcome has multiple causes, schools play a part. The differential performance of subject departments, schools, regions and nations in supporting similar groups of children is evidence that some are more effective than others in breaking the link between socioeconomic background and outcomes.

In this chapter we ask you to think about:

- school segregation and ability grouping
- the impact of expectations of learners
- working with learners' limited confidence and experience
- teaching and learning for all.

Case examples to illustrate points are drawn from four co-educational schools in England: Trichard Community Infants (5–7) in central London; Blackberry Primary (5–11), a small Church of England village school in eastern England; Elands (11–16), and Maclear (11–16) Community Schools, both in the south of England.

School segregation

In Chapter 2 we discussed how in the UK and many parts of Europe policy on school choice has resulted in greater segregation of learners by socio-economic status (Agirdag et al., 2012; Croxford, 2001): the more that learners are polarized by socioeconomic status, the more intense the effect on their learning. We recognize that segregation works in favour of many children and their families. Willms (2006) suggests that the advantages of a concentration of high SES intake to the individual learner are many. He suggests that such schools:

- have bright and motivated students who help each other learn
- find it easier to attract and retain talented teachers
- have greater support from parents
- have fewer disciplinary problems
- can teach to high standards and at a faster pace
- have smaller class sizes and better resources (adapted from Willms, 2006: 39–47).

They may also provide access to social networks that smooth their entry into work experience/internships, elite universities and jobs. By contrast, schools with a high concentration of low SES intake suffer from 'pupils' sense of futility and futility culture' (Agirdag et al., 2012: 366), which depresses their school's performance. Whilst Agirdag et al.'s results show a significant relationship between achievement and school composition – that is, the socioeconomic profile of learners – the analysis does not support a deterministic, negative view. Such schools are not doomed to low achievement. On the contrary, the findings suggest that a sense of futility can be overcome and a positive environment can support high levels of attainment.

Taking up his post, the head teacher of Elands School encountered something like Agirdag et al.'s futility culture:

Elands: learners' lack of confidence

They are very aware of what's lacking in their life and they tend to keep themselves to themselves and almost turn in on themselves. A student who takes a free school meal is very aware that they take a free school meal and what they do is they look at other students. They see others have a nicer bag and start to think 'I haven't got a nice bag. That's something that is lacking in my life'. I saw that more when I came here, given the school profile. The students are just as able, just as bright, just as keen to get on in their lives but the system as they perceive it is stacked against them.

It's about the culture of the school, emphasizing that 'you can do it'. When we are talking to students we talk about you can, you can do this. Very much what I would call neurolinguistic programming kind of techniques. You talk to students asking, 'where do you see yourself in ten years' and they are now much, much clearer in terms of saying what they want and how they see their life kind of panning out. OK, and so we say, 'what do you need to do to get there?'

This head teacher's insistence to students that they can do it echoes Obama's ringing statement to America in his presidential victory address, 'Yes we can', with the same intention. Undermining a sense of hopelessness and turning around the culture is a key responsibility of leaders. However, in itself, as somebody even as powerful as the president of the United States discovered, such belief is not enough. Multiple practical strategies are needed to counter the effects of poverty.

In-school segregation: ability grouping

Segregation is not just between but also within schools. Hallam and Parsons (2013) chart the history of streaming in primary schools in England. As discussed in Chapter 5, streaming is where children are placed in a class permanently on the basis of their perceived attainment. When there was a grammar school system throughout the UK, streaming was common in primary schools. The practice declined in the 1950s and 1960s, but since the 1990s streaming and setting – that is, placing children in ability groups for particular subjects – have grown steadily. Analysis of the millennium cohort study of children in the UK indicates that nearly one in five children is streamed at primary school level, and the percentage is higher at secondary level (Hallam and Parsons, 2013). There is little surprise that cognitive ability or prior attainment is only one of the predictors for placement in a top or bottom group. Hallam and Parsons (2013: 532) found that:

> Children in the top stream were most likely to live in an owner-occupied home (76.7%) and children in the bottom stream the least likely (40%). 13.2% of children in the top stream lived in local authority or housing association rented accommodation. This increased to 26.7% for children in the middle stream and 44.2% among children in the bottom stream.

Coming from a lone parent family was another significant predictor of being placed in the bottom stream.

Hallam and Ireson (2003) surveyed over 1,500 teachers in 45 secondary comprehensive schools in England, and uncovered a range of attitudes to the advantages of streaming/setting or mixed ability groups. More experienced teachers and those who teach the arts and humanities were more likely to be positive towards mixed ability than the less experienced and those who teach mathematics or languages. Science teachers, on average, hold a middle position.

Staff were aware of hierarchies created by setting that serve to disadvantage particular pupils, but in many cases were reluctant to establish mixed ability classes. The most able, as they saw it, would pay an unacceptably high price in terms of being held back. The cost of streaming or setting to those in lower attaining groups, the majority from disadvantaged backgrounds, often seems to be a lower priority concern. The research suggests a downward spiral where students placed in sets of lower attainment resist the resulting stigma with poor behaviour and effort, leading to demoralized and alienated teachers, which depresses attainment still further (Hallam et al., 2004).

The evidence of whether mixed ability groups have a negative impact on high-attaining individuals is unsatisfactory and contradictory (Hallam and Parsons, 2013). The varying ways classes are mixed and curriculum and pedagogy differentiated mean that research results are not directly comparable. However, there is clear evidence that, overall, attainment is greater and the education system gains by eliminating streaming. Hanushek (2006) uses PISA data from over 18 countries to consider the effects of streaming or setting before age 15, and concludes that it increases inequality, especially when it begins early in the system, and that there is little evidence to suggest that this results in an overall gain in performance across schools.

We have been referring to high-attaining and low-attaining groups, but this is a matter of convenience. As we have already suggested, the set a pupil ends up in is likely to be related not only to objective assessment of attainment but to socioeconomic status. Streaming or setting in both primary and secondary schools, in effect, recreates in miniature the segregation across schools by SES status.

There is a long history of teachers advocating streaming or setting, believing this allows them to teach more effectively. It is also usually less demanding. We would ask you to consider why, when there is evidence that they disadvantage further those from poor backgrounds and achieve no overall performance gains in the education system, setting and streaming persist.

Expectations of learners

From the mid-twentieth century onwards there have been three propositions in relation to teacher expectations. First, they are influenced by a range of factors, including socioeconomic background. Second, they are a stronger predictor of learner performance than those of the learner or parents, and third, they are self-fulfilling (Rubie-Davies et al., 2010).

Most teachers believe that their expectations of those from disadvantaged backgrounds are as high as for more advantaged pupils. White et al. (2014) surveyed 248 senior leaders and 915 classroom teachers in both primary and secondary schools in the UK. Regarding expectations, 17 per cent of primary school teachers and 26 per cent of secondary school teachers agreed that colleagues have lower expectations of students from disadvantaged backgrounds and that this has a negative impact on the outcomes of learners in this group. Whilst the majority believe expectations are uninfluenced by socioeconomic background, a significant minority of teachers – about one in four – observe colleagues, if not themselves, expecting less of the disadvantaged.

In several of the case example schools staff spoke about the critical nature of high expectations, but emphasized that this had to be more than a glib phrase. Each had a particular approach to what high expectations look like when embedded in practice. In several cases there was detailed and systematic tracking of each individual child to ensure they were achieving well. There was also a sense of the need to repeatedly challenge staff, who might otherwise slip back into lazy and prejudicial assessments that were intended to be supportive of children. Kindness can be just as deadly as negligence, leading to passive prejudice, in the words of the head teacher of Blackberry School:

Blackberry: passive prejudice

Prejudice can be somewhat 'passive', not born out of any feeling of superiority, but more as a result of lack of experience. However, prejudice, wherever it stems from, is equally damaging, so needs to be challenged at every level. Expectations need to be consistently high for all learners, but also school adults need to really understand the barriers and challenges that some families have in supporting children to arrive at school ready to learn, and this must be built in to the support systems and learning scaffolding that are put in place for all children.

Statements about high expectations may be just hype, unless tightly tied to a realistic understanding of the learning context of each child and the means to support him or her. Consequently, in Blackberry School the head teacher stressed the need to balance high expectations with well-planned structures in order to achieve them.

In Elands School children have very limited resources of any kind in their background. Embedding high expectations in this school uses a similar dual approach to that of Blackberry School. The head teacher tries to ensure that everybody understands what excellence means and relates this to a realistic understanding that everybody has to work harder, learners and staff, and deal with failure more frequently than in schools with children from more privileged backgrounds:

Elands: high expectations in practice

We often talk to students about what excellence looks like and how we model that and I call it the final 5 per cent. Actually you can give 95 per cent in any situation but it always seems to be the final 5 per cent that counts and that for me, that element, that is the difference between average and excellence, that final 5 per cent. So we often ask the students to go a little bit above and beyond in terms of what they want. I certainly ask the staff to go a little bit above and beyond, you know, what they think and try and work that through.

The values are a fundamental belief that anybody can go to university if they choose to do so. They've just got to work on this element of hard work and effort. And accepting if you are starting on the lower rung of the ladder it's going to be a little bit harder but it's not a reason why you cannot go. So actually teaching them all the soft skills about when something doesn't go your way, how do you deal with that, how do you cope with the concept of failure, taken that it is only a concept, it's not really something real. You know I still drive my car but I didn't pass my test the first time. Failure means that I would never get in a car again and never experience that, so we change how we say things and how we approach it.

So when we see a student outside lessons now instead of being in a classroom, we ask, 'What are you learning in the corridor?' not 'What have you been sent out for?' So they realize it's better to be in the lesson than outside. So these values are driven at senior management level through the line management structure, to not allow people to make any excuses about why students might not perform and do well.

In the words of the head teacher from Maclear School, 'It can be a cliché, can't it, but in the end it's about no glass ceilings and everyone, everyone, has the ability and the opportunity and the possibility. It is the key to unlocking that potential'.

The key point from these case examples is that opportunities and possibilities have to be created through practical actions to make a reality of high expectations. As discussed in Chapter 1, Sen's (1980) approach to justice focuses on capabilities; that is, what people are enabled to do. It is not just a question of recognizing abilities and potential but also of providing the context in which these can be used. It is no good providing a library of books when few have good reading skills. The head teachers quoted in the case examples above are consistent in their message: simply believing that children are capable of much more than we might imagine is merely a first step. Creating the opportunities for them to make the possibilities a reality is the make-or-break challenge for schools and needs to be understood by all staff.

Working with learners' limited confidence and experience

To children living in poverty, school staff may seem to come from another planet. They use a different language, and often have different interests and unfamiliar ways of behaving. Succeeding at school can sometimes seem like moving from one world to another. Children in poverty generally lack the social capital that is taken for granted by others. In Trichard School, the head teacher was well aware of the limited know-how of some children yet was still taken by surprise by what they have not experienced:

Trichard: social capital

We want to provide all children with engaging and challenging opportunities to learn. We aim to provide an oasis for some of the children, away from the rest of their lives, and want to guarantee each child a rich experience in terms of music, theatre and visits out of school. We once went to St Paul's and had an hour to spare and we walked them to the Tate Modern Museum over the footbridge. Some children had not seen a river before. They were born in London but had never seen a river!

Gaining social capital by adopting new ways of thinking and behaving can also seem to entail cutting ties with family. Moskal (2014) reports heartbreaking accounts from parents in Scotland of their children rejecting them as stupid, turning their back on their parents' way of life as they adapt to what is required to 'do well' at a school. Some take this path. Others choose to reject such change and stay within what they and their family know. To have genuine choice about their future, children from disadvantaged socioeconomic backgrounds need to engage with new and unfamiliar possibilities. They may react positively with excitement, but may also withdraw from what seems too far outside their experience, and so too frightening. One example comes from the head teacher of Elands School:

Elands: offering new experiences

In my first year, the Tall Ships charity contacted us and offered two free places to our students to have a week's sailing experience on a tall ship. I thought great! This really fits what we want to do but I couldn't get any students to go. It was so far out of their world. It was such a big leap. I found the students here very lacking in confidence to be able to think that they could leave home for five days, leaving mum or dad or step-dad, and live in a different environment.

The head teacher recognized that 'students should experience more in the real world than maybe they think they are entitled to', but just being offered the opportunity, as in the case of the Tall Ships, does not necessarily work. A persistent focus in this school is building confidence. On taking up the post the head teacher had asked the children if they intended to go to university. Very few responded positively. After several years' work on the children's confidence, about 50 per cent now entertain going to university as a possibility. Building children's confidence, their resilience and ability to cope is a long-term project.

There is a large and growing literature about resilience, buoyancy, well-being and children's strategies for coping with stress. Such research can increase understanding of how to help those children with the furthest distance to travel (Bailey, 2009; Harvey and Delfabbro, 2004; Martin and Marsh, 2008). Many studies find that children cope more positively if they have warm, supportive relationships with adults, a stable environment and opportunities to make decisions for themselves (Zimmer-Gembeck and Locke, 2007). Though teachers may intend these factors to be consistently present in school, there is much evidence from a minority of children, usually from disadvantaged socioeconomic backgrounds, that they experience the contrary (Lumby, 2012a). Many of this group can identify effective and caring teachers, yet also experience rejection, through repeated coercion and an emphasis on their incompetence (Hamill and Boyd, 2002; Riley et al., 2006).

In a comparative study of learners' views in Japan and England, 54 per cent in Japan and 41 per cent in England believed that all students are treated the same way in class. In both countries over 80 per cent believed teachers have favourites, particularly the students who work hard (Smith and Gorard, 2012). This recalls discussions in Chapter 1 about the 'Matthew effect'; teachers may not intend to favour the hard-working or able, but evidence suggests that many do. Building confidence in children who start far back demands an unremitting insistence on positive relationships between all staff and children, to support children's willingness to open up to the novel experiences and possibilities that the school provides. As the head teacher of Maclear School puts it, 'You will not on the whole find any adult in this school bellowing at children up and down corridors or shouting or chasing after them. It isn't the way we work'. Nevertheless, occasional instances persist and are tackled immediately and head on by talking to the member of staff concerned.

Teaching and learning for all

As is clear from our discussion so far, inclusive teaching involves shifting not only what teachers do, but also what they believe. In the Anglophone world, historically, teaching is based on belief in a bell-curve distribution of ability in each class, of 'the gifted and talented, the struggling and the just average' (DfES, 2005: 20). Other cultures adopt a different approach, seeing the issue not as a child's innate ability, but their willingness to work hard and the appropriateness and persistence of the teacher support offered (Foskett and Lumby, 2003). The point is that teachers' beliefs about learning are not definitive, but culturally shaped. For example, the Confucian influence evident in China's education system suggests that:

> Innate ability does not account for success or failure in education. Confucius was willing to take in anyone who wanted to be educated, and insisted that 'no distinctions should be made in dispensing education' (*youjiao wulei*). There is a strong belief that everyone is educable and capable of attaining perfection. Although differences in intelligence and ability are recognised, they are not viewed as determinants of educational achievement. (Hu, 2002: 98)

Western education systems sometimes look to learn from Asian successes, but without understanding or being able to replicate their foundation in a genuine, rather than a rhetorical, belief that all children are capable of attaining high standards.

Carrington et al. (2015) suggest that inclusive teaching means not only every child learning, but also feeling a valued member of the community. Many teachers might recognize the technical, pedagogic challenges in helping all children in their class learn. Ensuring every child feels valued may be more of a challenge because it is not a technical issue, but an ethical and social one. A narrative from a trainee teacher placed in a secondary school notes teachers' sympathy for those teachers allocated to 'bottom' sets or to discrete classes of disruptive students removed from the mainstream. He wonders whether such arrangements are to help the children concerned or the teachers (Magill and Rodriguez, 2015). This student teacher was aware from the beginning of training that not all children are valued equally.

Florian and Linklater (2010: 818) studied two Scottish primary schools, and suggest that teaching that is successful for all requires:

- a shift in focus from one that is concerned with only those individuals who have been identified as having 'additional needs', to learning for all – the idea of everybody (not most and some)
- a rejection of deterministic beliefs about ability (and the associated idea that the presence of some will hold back the progress of others)
- ways of working with and through other adults that respect the dignity of learners as full members of the community of the classroom.

This is a challenging agenda, but one offering ideas to transform schools in fundamental ways, tackling beliefs as well as practice. Exploring in detail teaching and learning to achieve such a shift is beyond the scope of a single chapter. There are also aspects of what needs to be done, such as working with parents and the community, and strengthening the advice given to children about their future pathways, which we have not been able to include here. However, starting points can be suggested. The additional reading below provides some practical ideas about strategies and pedagogies to achieve a school that includes all children, enabling them to thrive and grow into self-aware social beings and citizens, whatever their socioeconomic background.

The achievement gap

In her presidential address to the American Educational Research Association, Gloria Ladson-Billings compared the educational achievement gap between the rich and poor to a nation's economic deficit (Ladson-Billings, 2006). Many nations focus on the difference between their income and outgoings each year: the annual deficit. They are concerned to adjust the budget so that income and expenditure match. People can understand this concept and see such relatively small adjustments as 'doable' in the short term. In contrast, the national economic debt is a mountain of money, the result of accumulated deficits over very many years, and it is much harder to see how to fix. For some countries, it seems impossible to find a way to pay off a huge sum of money.

Schools are in an equivalent situation. The achievement gap resembles an annual deficit. The aim is to improve the figures in the short term. Just as the chancellor identifies what to cut, or new sources of taxation that will give a better outcome at the end of the financial year, so do schools seek quick fixes to improve their annual examination results. For example, they select learners on the borderline of grades and give them extra attention to boost results, or limit the enrolment of learners perceived as challenging, who might depress results.

The national debt, as opposed to the national deficit, requires much longer-term attention. To achieve sufficient savings to address the mountain of debt, the chancellor must habituate the nation to a huge shift, a different standard of living long term. Schools have an equivalent magnitude of debt caused by the historic persistent skewing of education towards the needs of the privileged. They, too, need a permanent alteration in ways of operating, involving fundamental changes in beliefs about learners and learning, the curriculum, assessment and pedagogy.

Neither in the economy nor in education has there been much willingness to address the necessary long-term changes. The education system has persisted in advantaging further those from advantaged backgrounds. As discussed in Chapter 1, schools often embody the 'Matthew effect': those who have more, gain more. Over the years, the debt of inequality has grown. Some suggest education merely reproduces the divisions in society and is not able to challenge them in any meaningful way. Our position is different. Schools may not be able to put right all inequalities, but research and practice have identified strategies that will bring about greater equality concerning how schools are structured, how teaching is delivered and how staff relate to learners. If we know much of what needs to be done to begin paying off the education debt, it is more a question of how much appetite there is for the task and how much courage and stamina to persist.

Key actions

- Avoid ability groupings as far as possible.
- Embed high expectations in multiple strategies:

  o provide professional development and support to build teachers' awareness of how beliefs about ability are culturally and socially formed, to counter misplaced assumptions of limited potential in some learners
  o build confidence in learners to make use of wider opportunities.

- Provide ongoing support to allow teachers to develop inclusive pedagogies with an emphasis on improving learning for all.

For reflection and discussion

How would you assess your school's progress in meeting the needs of students from disadvantaged socioeconomic backgrounds? Does the school locate responsibility for failures to learn and achieve with the learner and his or her family or, at least in part, with structures and teaching in the school?

Additional reading

For further reading on segregation, tracking, streaming and setting:

Bohlmark, A. and Lindahl, M. (2007) 'The impact of school choice on pupil achievement, segregation and costs: Swedish evidence', IZA Discussion Papers, No. 2786. www.econstor.eu/bitstream/10419/34645/1/555455319.pdf (accessed 27.11.15).

Gamoran, A. (2010) 'Tracking and inequality', in M. Apple, S. Ball and L.A. Gandin (eds), *The Routledge Handbook of the Sociology of Education*. London: Routledge, pp. 213–28.

Hallam, S. and Ireson, J. (2003) 'Secondary school teachers' attitudes towards and beliefs about ability grouping', *British Journal of Educational Psychology*, 73 (3): 343–56.

Hallam, S., Ireson, J. and Davies, J. (2004) 'Primary pupils' experiences of different types of grouping in school', *British Educational Research Journal*, 30 (4): 515–33.

For further reading on leading school cultures that are inclusive of those from socioeconomically disadvantaged backgrounds:

Ainscow, M. and Sandill, A. (2010) 'Developing inclusive education systems: the role of organisational cultures and leadership', *International Journal of Inclusive Education*, 14 (4): 401–16.

Cooper, P. (2002) *Effective Schools for Disaffected Students: Integration and Segregation*. London: Routledge.

Furman, G. and Shields, C. (2005) 'How can educational leaders promote and support social justice and democratic community in schools?', in W.A. Firestone and C. Riehl (eds), *A New Agenda for Research in Educational Leadership*. New York: Teachers College Press, pp. 119–37.

For further reading on inclusive classroom practices:

Florian, L. and Linklater, H. (2010) 'Preparing teachers for inclusive education: using inclusive pedagogy to enhance teaching and learning for all', *Cambridge Journal of Education*, 40 (4): 369–86.

Hayes, D., Johnston, K. and King, A. (2009) 'Creating enabling classroom practices in high poverty contexts: the disruptive possibilities of looking in classrooms', *Pedagogy, Culture and Society*, 17 (3): 251–64.

Macleod, S., Sharp, C., Bernardinelli, D., Skipp, A. and Higgins, S. (2015) *Supporting the Attainment of Disadvantaged Pupils: Articulating Success and Good Practice*. London: DfE. www.gov.uk/government/uploads/system/uploads/attachment_data/file/473974/DFE-RR411_Supporting_the_attainment_of_disadvantaged_pupils.pdf (accessed 30.11.15).

7

Gender and equality

Gender pervades all that we do and, along with other characteristics, has an impact on the educational success and experience of school, for both students and staff. This chapter focuses on the ways in which gender might advantage or disadvantage students and how best to support each individual to be equipped for life. Gender issues affect adults in schools as well as students (see pp. 44–5), particularly women who aspire to leadership positions in schools, or men who wish to work in education for young children. Suggestions for further reading in these two areas are made at the end of this chapter.

In this chapter we ask you to think about:

- how we develop gender identity
- our understanding of the attainment gap between girls and boys
- ways of narrowing the attainment gap
- how gender affects the experience of school
- ways in which we can counter the negative impact of gender stereotypes.

Case examples have been drawn from three schools: Tulback Academy (co-educational 11–18) in inner London; Willis Girls', an independent all-age school in southern England; and Revel Girls' Academy (11–18) in inner London.

Establishing a gender identity

Children learn steadily about gender from birth. They learn through their family and community, from their peer group, and from the nursery and school environment. Although there are proponents of innate brain difference between the genders, as neuro-science develops the evidence is mounting that environment and social interaction play the biggest part in gender identity formation (Francis, 2006). Development of masculine and feminine identities is 'essentially a cognitive process' (Paechter, 2007: 2), and a child's understanding of what it means to be male and female then drives his or her behaviour. Establishing a gender identity, therefore, is not a once-and-for-all process but something that is dynamic, involving us in performing 'male' or 'female' in a variety of ways that can change over time. Gender is not necessarily fixed, and particular support may be needed for those who are questioning their gender or are transgender, and in Chapter 8 we will look at issues relating specifically to sexual identity.

There is a stereotypical way of performing 'male', which is to be macho, powerful, strong, aggressive, competitive, sporty and uninterested in study, but not all boys and men conform to this image, and many find it restricting and uncomfortable. For example, there are studious boys who may be labelled 'geeks' (Ward, 2014), also 'caring, sharing boys' (Younger and Warrington, 2005: 5) who exemplify alternative ways of performing/being a young male. For girls, there is a stereotypical image of a quiet and compliant student who works hard academically, always behaves 'nicely', looks feminine and pretty, tends not to participate in sports and takes a supportive rather than a leadership role. The latter part of this stereotype is enhanced by the fact that women are noticeably less well represented in positions of power in society (EHRC, 2011). Despite the prevailing stereotype, there are many different ways of performing 'girl', including exhibiting 'girl power' or being a 'mean girl'.

From this, it is obvious that we should not essentialize boys and girls; that is, assume that each group displays the same characteristics. In addition, as discussed in Chapter 3, the process of identity formation means that gender intersects with other characteristics, for example ethnicity, class and religion, each of which carries its own stereotypes and expectations. What is important is that people in schools are aware of and can confront the ways in which gender and other stereotypes can limit academic and career possibilities for both girls and boys, and consequently career chances for women and men. Also, if schools are to prepare children to 'live a life they value' (see Chapter 1), they have a duty to counter the harmful effects of gender stereotypes on students' emotional health and well-being.

The gender attainment gap

In the UK and elsewhere there is a great deal of media coverage of the gap in attainment between boys and girls that focuses narrowly on examination results. For example, in England and Wales there are regular headlines about GCSE and A-level results, such as: 'Girls pulling further ahead of boys' (in relation to GCSE results), or 'Gender gap between boys and girls closing' (in relation to A-level results). Both of these headlines appeared in the *Daily Telegraph* in August 2014 (Paton, 2014). How do gender identity stereotypes contribute to this debate?

Following equal opportunities legislation in the 1980s there was an emphasis on anti-sexist measures and equal opportunities for girls (Maguire, 2006), but more recently the focus has shifted to the relative academic success of girls in public examinations and the fact that they are more likely than boys to go to university. Their success, which goes against traditional gender stereotypes, has then sometimes been seen as a 'threat' to boys' achievement, and the assumption is that education has been feminized, disadvantaging boys. The focus on boys has also given support to a view that gender inequality for girls is no longer a problem. The narrow focus on exam results also means that little attention is given to achieving student well-being or to any other type of educational achievement, including a successful preparation for life. Even within the narrow focus of the exam results, the particular concern with the success of girls and apparent under-achievement of boys means that sight of other aspects of the results is lost, for example:

- the examination performance of boys as well as girls is steadily improving
- not all girls do well and not all boys do badly in examinations
- boys' under-achievement would be better measured by value-added rather than examination results
- girls actually achieved better than boys in the old 11+ examination and in O-levels, so their success is not new
- there is major international concern about girls' relatively poor achievement in maths. (OECD, 2014b)

Importantly, the narrow focus on the gender gap draws attention away from the fact that socioeconomic class and ethnicity are both factors that account for more difference in examination results than gender. Students from better-off families are much more likely to achieve good examination grades than those with poorer socioeconomic circumstances, and some ethnic groups consistently do better than others. Class, ethnicity and gender intersect to mean that, in the UK overall, it is White working-class boys who generally achieve less well than other groups. Although the media tend to focus on the gender dimension, White working-class girls do little better. The deputy head teacher of Tulback School commented on how little difference there was between the boys and girls:

Tulback: White working-class boys and girls

There has been a tremendous focus on White working-class boys, but White working-class girls also present a big problem. White working-class boys become NEETS [not in employment, education or training] but White working-class girls who also perform fairly poorly can become pregnant. Although the discourse about boys has diminished it [girls' under-achievement] is no less of an issue.

Is there an international gender attainment gap?

Concern about a gender gap in academic attainment is not limited to the UK. The same concerns are experienced in the USA (Grogan and Dias, 2015) and in Europe (Delhaxhe, 2009) and, in both cases, despite the anxiety about boys' apparently poorer academic achievement, gender is again a less significant factor than socioeconomic circumstances. Nevertheless, there is concern about boys who, on average at age 15, achieve less well in PISA tests; 14 per cent of 15-year-old boys against 9 per cent of girls do not reach the base level of proficiency in reading, maths and science, and there is also concern about girls' performance in science and maths (OECD, 2015a). Again, it is necessary to look beyond the headlines. There is wide variation between countries, indicating that differences between boys and girls are not inevitable, but are 'avoidable outcomes of social and cultural differences' (Delhaxhe, 2009: 44).

What about the girls?

Although girls generally achieve better academically and gain more places in higher education than boys, their apparent advantage disappears as they move through the life course with, for example, a continuing gender pay gap in the UK that was 19 per cent in 2014 (Fawcett Society, 2015). Socially and culturally, the education of girls is often regarded as less important than the education of boys. Girls and women tend to be identified with domestic responsibilities, so girls are more likely to experience 'parentally condoned absences, low aspirations, caring responsibilities and sexual exploitation' (Younger and Warrington, 2005: 58), and this gendered experience intersects with class, ethnicity and religion so that it is felt much more keenly by some than others.

Although both boys and girls are subject to sexual exploitation, girls are more often the target of sexual grooming by older males, and may be sexually harassed by both older men and their male classmates. Bullying and other unpleasant repercussions around sexting are more commonly experienced by girls than boys (Ringrose et al., 2013), as are eating disorders and self-harm, although these are not restricted to girls. In addition, girls are more subject than boys to media and consumer pressures that encourage early sexualization. The head teacher of Willis School was aware that the challenge of early sexualization was one that was faced by her students:

Willis: Girls and sexualization

Sexualization of young people is a major challenge for parents, schools and communities, but is less so in a girls' school. I am not saying that things like sexting do not exist, but there is more of a sense of wholesomeness, of maintaining childhood. Girls can be girls in a single-sex environment where they can focus on interests, aspirations and study, and generally don't feel overly pressured to impress others, for example few wear makeup. When Year 11 girls finish their GCSE exams, they celebrate by playing on the junior school play equipment, enjoying moments from childhood.

There are arguments for and against single-sex schools and, in particular, there are parents who would prefer their daughters to attend such schools, often for religious or social reasons. However, there is little research to show that single-sex schools produce better examination results than co-educational schools, that girls attending single-sex schools are more or less interested in boys, or that the attitudes of both sexes to career equity are affected (Leonard and Murphy, 2007).

There remain important issues for girls regarding gendered subject choice. Looking more closely at the examination results in the UK, it is apparent that there are large gender differences in the take-up of different subjects. At A-level, twice as many boys than girls study maths, and four times more boys than girls study physics, whilst double the number of girls than boys study English (Paton, 2014). Such gendered subject choices have enormous implications for future careers and potential earnings, and schools are aware of the importance of encouraging girls to study science, technology, engineering and maths (STEM) subjects. The deputy head of Tulback School regarded this as a key area in gender equality:

Tulback: gendered subject choice

We are very aware of girls not taking science at A-level. It is an area where we see the most stereotyping and we are challenging those stereotypes. We work with a local engineering firm who have been working with students, particularly girls, encouraging them into science and engineering careers. That's one initiative. The science department is largely female and they are targeting girls to look at careers in science. One science teacher got a female engineer to talk to girls.

Equally, it is important that boys are not constrained by gendered expectations that restrict their choice of 'female' subjects such as literature and languages, or caring careers, or access to sporting opportunities of every kind. Gendered subject choices start to occur early and are well recognized (Myers and Taylor, 2007), due largely to social and cultural pressures that affect gender identity formation. In a study across European countries, Iannelli and Smyth (2008) found that there was no common pattern in how gender impacted on educational and later career success as it depended on the interplay of many factors, only one of which was subject choice. The message is that gender need not be destiny.

Gender identity and schools

The focus in English schools is on fairly narrowly defined academic achievement, rather than, for example, vocational preparation. Recent policy changes have reinforced this, as indicated in Chapter 2. The system is therefore set up to reward those who can achieve academic success (more likely to be middle class and female) and to fail those who cannot (more likely to be working class and male). In her study of 'lads and ladettes', Jackson (2006) points out that young people may act to build defences against failure and one way of doing this is to reject academic work, often regarded as 'feminine', and to develop a 'laddish' identity in which social pursuits are seen as more important than schoolwork. Although laddish behaviour is generally a masculine construct, such behaviour may be adopted by some girls, who also might be seeking a way of avoiding the high-stakes culture of pure academic success. Whilst laddish behaviour is linked with boys' under-achievement, the perceived academic success of girls overall means that it is the transgression of gender boundaries, rather than academic failure, that tends to be emphasized for 'ladettes' (Jackson, 2006: 142).

Although we cannot essentialize the nature of boys and girls, there are culturally and socially influenced generalities that can be observed. For example, research in countries reporting data to PISA indicates that, in general, boys are much less likely to read for pleasure than girls, much more likely to spend time on computer games and the Internet, and spend less time on homework (OECD, 2015a). Boys are generally perceived by girls to be immature and disruptive in class, although the girls may recognize that the boys might be acting out a role to impress their mates and are not so brash when talking one-to-one (Younger and Warrington, 2005). The same research found that boys of 15 years tend to be over-confident, even arrogant, about their ability to do well in examinations, irrespective of the amount of work they actually do. They tend to refuse to accept responsibility for their own progress or lack of it, whilst the girls tend to be much more cautious and realistic about the amount of work they should be doing. Typically, therefore, boys display over-confidence whilst girls tend to under-estimate their abilities and over-react to criticism or perceived failure. In the following example, the deputy head teacher of Tulback School compared her experiences of working in a mixed and an all-boys school:

Tulback: girls and boys in the classroom

The big difference is how they respond to praise and criticism. Boys want public affirmation; they like to be complimented publicly whilst girls do not. Instead, they like a quiet word. I think that sometimes male teachers in particular find it hard to understand why girls don't respond to praise and respond so negatively to criticism – they may need to adjust their practice. There is also a difference in how much boys and girls remember. Boys are more confident in being told off and forget quickly whilst girls tend to remember such incidents much longer.

Girls continue to have a generally poorer academic self-concept than boys, although the effect of single-sex schooling does appear to counter this tendency to a limited extent (Sullivan, 2009).

Gender stereotypes can impact on the well-being and emotional health of students. In the following examples from two very different girls' schools there is awareness of the need to address confidence issues for girls. The first concerns girls whose identity is built on high achievement and potentially unrealistic expectations of continuous success in the context of an independent girls' school:

Willis: self-esteem

Self-esteem is vitally important, and enables them to be resilient and to manage failure. In an academic school like this, that is particularly important. I have a tea party in my room for them when they fail the driving test, as it is the first time they have failed at anything. Clever girls can be fragile learners and not necessarily good at dealing with failure, not good at having a Plan B. When they apply to Oxbridge, I say that is great, but what is Plan B? We try to show them that there is not always a right answer to everything. We try and teach them twenty-first century skills, teamwork, creative problem solving, etc. and we have focus weeks on these. We encourage risk taking in their learning and we want to develop them as confident young women capable of changing the world, and to be able to manage themselves and their careers as they learn to be comfortable with change.

The second example concerns girls who are mainly from a working-class background, where they may lack social capital. Many are from a minority ethnic background where their religious identity is important. In both of these very different examples, it is apparent that gendered expectations manifested through a lack of confidence are an issue and that both schools are taking action to counter this, contributing to learners' development as a whole:

Revel: self-esteem

We do a lot of work on confidence building. We call it Young Leadership and from the start make opportunities for girls to be Young Leaders or

Ambassadors, we tend to call them. We are always giving out Leap Awards (a young leadership programme). They are presented as a challenge and an opportunity. For example, in Year 7 they go back to their primary school and talk there about being in senior school. In the Leap Leadership awards, for example, there are ten challenges to get a bronze award, e.g. visit a library, read three books in a term, have a conversation with an adult. As it goes on to silver and gold, it gets more challenging, e.g. do a voluntary activity, be a tour guide for visitors and they may become a prefect. We also have sports leaders, dance leaders and language leaders. They might do assemblies; the older ones get on the platform with me and give speeches. There is a lot of debating and emphasis on the spoken word. We have a termly concert where poets, musicians and dancers have the opportunity to be on the stage. It is a strong part of our school culture. The idea is that all take part.

Countering gender stereotypes and fostering appropriate levels of confidence are very important for girls, but it is also important to counter the unhelpful gender stereotypes attached to boys, which have the effect of limiting them emotionally as well as academically. Whilst girls may be more subject to eating disorders and self-harm, the suicide rate for boys massively outstrips that of girls. For the 15 to 19 age group in 2013, there were 131 male suicides and 31 female suicides in the UK (Samaritans, 2015).

Narrowing the academic achievement gap

Boys can be trapped by the macho images to which they are expected to live up, which may divert them from enjoying the benefits from the education offered to them. Working within the admittedly narrow limits of the gender academic achievement gap, four approaches or interventions have been identified. Younger and Warrington (2005) advocate looking at: pedagogy, particularly teaching, learning and assessment styles; individual approaches including mentoring and target setting; organizational strategies or attempts to change the whole-school ethos and culture; and socio-cultural approaches specifically aimed at laddish behaviour.

In particular, it is thought that coursework has favoured feminine ways of working, that the curriculum might be made more 'boy friendly', particularly with regard to reading matter, and that the absence of male role models in primary schools might be damaging to boys' education. However, there is little evidence that a particular learning style is favoured by boys or girls. Trials in a number of schools have shown that individual learning styles change over time and are not particularly related to gender (DCSF, 2009; Younger and Warrington, 2005). The most successful strategies have involved awareness of different learning styles, and encouragement to pupils to be more aware of their own learning and what works best for them, and this applies to girls just as much as to boys. There is some evidence that single-sex teaching can work well, although conclusions from the research indicate a danger that it can simply reinforce gender stereotypes and that what is successful is high quality teaching. Both sexes said that what they wanted was:

> well-organized and clearly structured lessons, clear teacher explanations and a willingness to take a different perspective if students did not understand something, a choice of activities, encouragement, variety, more discussion and a disciplined, though not authoritarian, classroom environment. (Younger and Warrington, 2005: 51)

Although girls tend to be better than boys at reading and writing, and this might favour them in terms of coursework, there is evidence to show that girls had already improved their achievement before the introduction of coursework and that they tend to perform well in end-of-course examinations (DCSF, 2009). In the example below, the deputy head of Tulback School reflected on how gender differences work out in practice:

Tulback: girls and boys learning differently

I can get boys to work in groups and to work individually and I have not found particular differences in the ways that boys and girls do coursework now they have been doing it for so long. There are some differences in concentration, as girls tend to be more focused, but of course that is not true all of the time. People do find teaching boys is different from teaching girls and ideally you adopt a range of styles and strategies: where teachers are able to do that they don't notice the differences so much. We have discussions at school level about how girls and boys learn differently and five years ago it was all about boys and boys' achievement, but it is not so high on the agenda any more.

Boys lag behind girls in reading, and it is suggested that boy-friendly reading material, including more non-fiction, would be beneficial to them. The danger here, again, is that we might unwittingly conform to and reinforce existing gender stereotypes. The evidence seems to indicate that a wide range of suggested reading matter that does not limit choice is good for both boys and for girls, and that what helps to raise achievement and reduce the gender gap is high expectations for all (DCSF, 2009).

The relevance of the gender of the teacher to the success of the pupil has focused on the absence of male teachers in the primary classroom. However, a quantitative study (Carrington et al., 2008) found no evidence that male teachers improve the academic outcomes of boys, but that the absence of male role models may impact in other ways, and acknowledged that the influence of gender on classroom interactions between teachers and pupils is complex. Part of that interaction might relate to the gender of those who lead the school and, in secondary schools, there is a disproportionate bias towards male leaders (see further reading suggestions at the end of this chapter).

Countering the negative impact of gender stereotypes

There is a range of strategies that can be successfully applied to counter gender stereotyping that might affect the life chances of boys and girls in schools. This includes the establishment of a gender policy; ensuring that professional development considers gender issues; consideration of all aspects of curriculum including subject choice, the hidden curriculum, and sex and relationship education; careful monitoring of data relating to gender; and the provision of mentors and role models.

A gender policy

It is easy to disregard the subtlety of gender issues and how they may impact on all members of the school. It may be helpful to have a formal policy with regard to gender equality and regular, focused professional development for staff. The reported academic success of girls may otherwise lead to an unthinking assumption that there is no problem for girls and an unquestioning attitude to boys' under-achievement. Research with head teachers indicates that they are not always aware of the impact of gender (Fuller, 2013). Gender awareness involves questioning the applicability of stereotypes about the learning of girls and boys, and the future career choices they might make, as well as the career progress of women. Gendered assumptions about laddishness ignore the possible shortcomings of a narrowly focused view of what constitutes success in education, favouring those who have benefited from the 'Matthew effect' (see Chapter 1) and ignoring the possibility that there are other types of success. Schools will also have to consider the dynamic nature of social media and its implications for cyber-bullying and sexting, and how best to offer guidance for students.

Gender and the curriculum

It is necessary to counter the impact of gendered thinking on all aspects of the curriculum. There are obvious examples such as encouraging girls to take STEM subjects, ensuring that boys do not see English and modern languages as female-only options, and valuing vocational as well as academic subjects, but there is also the hidden curriculum. This includes the distribution of responsibilities amongst male and female students and staff, and both Willis Girls' and Revel Girls' schools demonstrate good practice in relation to building confidence in girls. The school environment plays a part. Tulback School models good practice in breaking down stereotypes relating to gender and status, for example in the provision of toilets, avoiding traditional arrangements that could be sites for bullying and other anti-social activities. Instead, the toilets are gender-neutral and individually sited in communal areas for the use of both students and staff.

A relatively neglected aspect of the curriculum is that of relationship and sex education. This is criticized in the UK as being inconsistent in comparison with coverage in Scandinavian countries (Weale, 2015), yet can play a vital part in increasing awareness and understanding of gender issues, preparing students for more than academic life and indeed for living a life they value.

Monitoring and the collection of data

A key strategy in countering gender stereotypes is the collection and monitoring of data, relating not only to achievement but also to other indicators such as how gender relates to exclusions, attendance, special educational needs and subject choice. The second example from Revel School quoted in Chapter 3 (p.32) shows just how personalized this can be, monitoring not only the main parameters such as academic progress, ethnicity and students in receipt of pupil premium but also, for example, how many attend a sports club.

Mentoring and role models

Mentoring, coaching and the provision of role models are vital in breaking through gender barriers and raising aspirations at any stage of life, and mentoring techniques can be used both in relation to raising boys' achievement and motivation, and in providing career guidance for girls and boys. The one-to-one focus of mentoring is a particular strength of this strategy:

Tulback: mentoring

In the sixth form we work with a large management consultancy on a programme for children whose parents did not go to university and they are mentored for two years to get the guidance they need. During this time they also go to Cambridge for a weekend and are exposed to aspirational career guidance. It has been really helpful in terms of their university applications. We also work with the management consultancy to mentor under-achieving pupils in Year 11 and they are working with me in Year 9. We have external mentoring for girls who are not confident. The people from the consultancy are mainly female so that helps to raise the aspirations of some of our girls.

Although there have been considerable advances in gender equality, there is still subtle discrimination that disadvantages girls and women. There is also concern in most countries about the academic achievement of boys. Gender remains a pervasive and important factor when it comes to individuals achieving their educational potential, and it is incumbent on schools to ensure that gender is not a source of inequality.

Key actions

- Identify and counter gender stereotypes that affect how we learn, what subjects we study, our career choices and our emotional well-being.
- Work towards excellence of teaching providing a full range of opportunities for all pupils – girls and boys – in helping them to understand their own learning needs and responsibilities.

- Collect and monitor data of all kinds relating to gender issues, and implement appropriate intervention where helpful.
- Provide gender-aware mentoring, coaching and role models to foster appropriate levels of confidence and aspiration amongst boys and girls.

For reflection and discussion

A gender audit of staff would include, amongst others things: data on leadership responsibilities of staff; membership of the governing body; and policies and practice relating to recruitment and access to professional development. If you were aiming to eliminate gender stereotypes and potential discrimination, what might you include in a gender audit of the student body?

Additional reading

Two useful summaries that also critique simplistic interpretations of the gender attainment gap are:

DCSF (2009) *Gender and Education: Mythbusters*, http://webarchive.national archives.gov.uk/20130401151715/http://www.education.gov.uk/publications/ eOrderingDownload/00599-2009BKT-EN.pdf (accessed 15.08.15).

Boys' under-achievement:

GEA www.genderandeducation.com/resources/contexts/the-boys-underachieve ment-debate/ (accessed 08.05.16).

The references above are useful sources of information, and a most helpful summary of research relating to boys in school is still:

Younger, M. and Warrington, M. (2005) *Raising Boys' Achievement in Secondary Schools*. Maidenhead: Open University Press.

For further reading on women's access to leadership positions in schools, a good summary that remains relevant is:

Coleman, M. (2007) 'Gender and educational leadership in England: a comparison of secondary head teachers' views over time', *School Leadership and Management*, 27 (5): 383–99.

A more recent book that engages with concepts of leadership, gender, class and ethnicity in a feminist context is:

Fuller, K. (2013) *Gender, Identity and Educational Leadership.* London: Blooms-bury.

For further reading on men working in the area of early years education, a recent article is:

Mistry, M. and Sood, K. (2015) 'Why are there still so few men within Early Years in primary schools? Views from male trainee teachers and male leaders', *Education 3–13*, 43 (2): 115–27.

8

Sexuality and equality

As young people progress through school, potentially the most difficult and sensitive challenge they face is establishing their sexual identity. This is true for everyone, but particularly so for any young person who is perceived as being different from the heterosexual norm. This chapter focuses on sexuality and its potential relationship to equality in schools, mainly on how homophobic attitudes might impact on students' experience of school and their ability to benefit from their education. We consider the ways in which school leaders might promote policy and practice to ensure equality, and to establish an ethos where all students are equally valued, irrespective of their sexuality. As with all aspects of potential inequality, individual experiences will differ as equalities intersect. For example, there are particular sensitivities allied to some religious beliefs relating to those who do not conform to a heterosexual norm.

The related and large area of child protection and safeguarding is not covered in this chapter, but relevant references to guidelines on these topics are given in the further reading section.

In this chapter we ask you to think about:

- how sexuality relates to equality in schools
- the homophobic attitudes and discrimination experienced by lesbian, gay, bisexual and transgender (LGBT) students and staff and the underlying reasons for these attitudes
- policy and practice for equality relating to sexuality in two case example schools, and how these compare to policy and practice in your school.

Case examples are from two schools, each with good policy and practice on equality and sexuality: Winburg Academy (11–18) in southern England; and Glentanna Community Primary (5–11) in Scotland. Both are Stonewall champions (www.stonewall.org.uk/schoolchampions) and co-educational.

Some definitions

At this stage it may be useful to define the terms 'sex', 'gender' and 'sexuality'. 'Sex' is biologically defined in relation to reproductive organs as male, female or, in relatively rare cases, intersex (evidence of both male and female reproductive organs). 'Gender' is generally thought of as how an individual presents themselves to others in terms of masculinity and femininity, based mainly on their social experience. For transgender people, gender identity is not experienced as being the same as their biological identity and they may therefore choose to have treatment, including surgery, to change their body. 'Sexuality' relates particularly to 'an individual's tendencies, preferences and desires with respect to romantic partners and intimate relationships' (Meyer, 2010: 48).

How might sexuality affect equality in schools?

The development of gender and sexual identity is a particularly sensitive area for all young people, but for those who are questioning their sexuality, or who already identify as LGBT, the sensitivities are even greater. Girls and boys are expected to conform to gender and sex stereotypes as they mature, and those who transgress and do not fit gender stereotypes can experience homophobic bullying and exclusion by peers. LGBT members of staff may also encounter homophobic attitudes in the classroom, the staffroom and when it comes to promotion. One teacher commented: 'If I hadn't been so resilient and hadn't had the support of my head teacher I might not have stayed on' (Teacher Support Network, 2014: 2).

Sexuality affects equality when prejudice about sexuality limits the individual's access to education or employment/progress in education through discrimination, bullying and exclusion. In the UK, the age of sexual consent for homosexual as well as heterosexual acts has been established since 2001 at 16 years, and discrimination on the grounds of sexuality has been illegal since 2003. Despite the law, attitudes are slow to change and the sensitivities surrounding sexuality create challenges for school leaders to ensure that the culture of their school is inclusive to all, including LGBT students and staff.

Bullying, whether physical or psychological, of those seen as outsiders, has negative consequences on their mental and emotional health, self-esteem, school attendance and consequent academic performance. Although it is difficult to obtain definitive figures, it seems that LGBT young people are more likely to experience bullying than their heterosexual peers (Ofsted, 2012; Warwick et al., 2004). Homophobic bullying ranges from name-calling and ostracizing to physical abuse. A recent study identified:

- verbal bullying: being teased or called names
- rumour-mongering
- being compared to LGB or T (lesbian, gay, bisexual or transgender) celebrities, caricatures or characters that portray particular stereotypes of LGB or T people
- threat of being exposed (or 'outed') to friends and family as LGB or T, even when this is an incorrect perception
- being ignored or left out (i.e. indirect bullying or social exclusion)
- the use of inappropriate sexual gestures
- physical bullying: hitting, punching, kicking, sexual assault and threatening behaviour.

All of the above, with the exception of actual physical bullying, can also happen via email, text and on social networking sites (i.e. cyber-bullying) (Mitchell et al., 2014: 13).

It is not actually being gay that necessarily results in bullying, however. The whole notion of 'gay' may be a negatively perceived stereotype. Perhaps a fairly typical example of continuing low-level but nevertheless exclusionary and destructive behaviour is the experience of this gay teenager, looking back on his schooldays at college:

> Towards the end of being there I stopped making a conscious effort to fit in 'cos from one person calling me gay it went round all the school. Not that I was acting gay but if I was walking round the playground and someone saw me they would call me names and stuff and then just everyone was saying it because that's what everyone had been saying for ages. They were just saying it and labelling me as gay even if I came in straight as anything. (Vicars, 2006: 354)

Trying to eliminate bullying and low-level homophobic behaviour is necessary but not sufficient in leading for equality in relation to sexuality. There is a need to move beyond the assumption of heteronormativity; that is, that heterosexual relationships are the norm. Teachers working on action research projects to bring about change relating to homophobic attitudes in a primary school stated that:

we share the view, which is not necessarily expressed in all anti-bullying discourses around homophobia, that teachers need to reach beyond passive and disingenuous tolerance of 'those LGBT people' to proactively incorporate discussion of sexuality and gender into their curriculum. (De Palma and Atkinson, 2009: 839)

In relation to sexuality, perhaps the biggest challenge for educational leaders is to create a truly inclusive culture. This culture respects all members of the community and allows the visibility of LGBT students and staff within the school, valuing and welcoming individuals equally, and countering homophobic attitudes, bullying and a culture of heteronormativity. It is exemplified in the following quote:

Winburg: establishing an inclusive ethos

I want to work in an organization where people are confident to talk about lifestyle choices and to celebrate them and to talk them through with students. Secondary schools find it difficult to tackle sexuality, transgender, gay and lesbian issues. They find it difficult to say that they find it difficult, but they do. Schools tend not to tackle issues head on.

From an early age we need to challenge wherever we hear people speaking in derogatory terms about others. It cannot be left unchallenged. Sometimes you may meet opposition from parents who may see what you do as promoting LGBT issues. These issues need addressing sensitively from the beginning.

We have gay teachers here also who are happy to talk about it and we make it a priority. It has taken five years for them to feel comfortable. We have had two civil ceremonies which have been celebrated here and people see it as something we are proud to celebrate. We do not want to be an organization that hides people away. Think about the damage that does to young people who are gay or unsure about their sexuality. It is so destructive if they cannot feel free to talk. Two staff came and asked if they could talk to students about being gay. There have been no complaints from parents, but if there were, we would tackle it.

Dealing with issues of sexuality may be particularly sensitive with primary age pupils. In the case example that follows, the head teacher and senior teacher commented on the concept of inclusion in relation to attitudes to students and the wider community:

Glentanna: establishing an inclusive ethos

In today's culture it is important to look at diversity and inclusion and for young people to be able to speak freely of their family and environment. Inclusion is extremely important here.

This is life. There must be children in the school who are gay. They need to be represented and protected. We are not explicit in addressing sexuality with the children but just raising issues of diversity in the world; that everyone is different.

We are able to make direct links [for the children] because there are diverse families in the school and this makes the policy more tangible. That is an advantage of having a big [primary] school. We have children who are looked after, children living with grandparents and aunts as well as children with same-sex parents. We give children opportunities to talk about their own life and ensure it is a comfortable environment for them to do so.

The extent of homophobic attitudes

Currently about 6 per cent of the population are thought to be LGBT (Stonewall, undated), but the impact of homophobic bullying extends to others, including students who do not identify as LGBT but who may be academically high-achieving and serious about their studies. This might apply particularly to boys who, in response to gay taunts, adopt laddish behaviour that affects their chances of academic success (Francis et al., 2010). Other students who are likely to be affected by the use of homophobic language include those whose parents or carers are LGBT and, indeed, any child or young person who is perceived to be 'different'. There are 'deeply embedded processes which offer barriers to diversity and inclusion in education' (Lumby with Coleman, 2007: 42). Such processes maintain the superiority of the dominant group by labelling and stereotyping those seen as outsiders, and this defensive behaviour may be especially relevant during adolescence, when gender and sexual identity are fragile and in the process of being established.

It may be thought that homophobia is mainly found in the secondary and tertiary sector of education, but there is evidence of homophobic bullying in the primary phase of schooling. A Stonewall report in 2014 found that, whilst only half of primary teachers were aware of it, homophobic bullying had been observed by nearly nine out of ten secondary teachers

(Mitchell et al., 2014). In another Stonewall publication (Guasp et al., 2014) it is reported that three-quarters of primary school teachers hear the phrase 'you are so gay' or 'that is so gay' at school. Stonewall also indicates that addressing homophobic issues with older primary age students may be the ideal time to influence attitudes. At Glentanna School a teacher commented on the use of discriminatory language before and after the school undertook a change in practice related to sexuality:

Glentanna: the importance of language

I was aware that homophobic insults were used in the school and were not being challenged. I felt that I should challenge, but had no guidance and did not know if I would be supported.

You used to hear things like: 'your shoes are so gay'. You just don't hear that sort of thing anymore, or if you do you are more confident in challenging it. After all, the children may not know that certain language is inappropriate. Now we can have a discussion about what words mean and how they can be used.

Sensitivity in relation to sexual orientation is particularly strong in adolescence, yet homophobic attitudes, exclusion and bullying may also be experienced by the adults in schools. The Teacher Support Network (2014: 2) reported that 48 per cent of LGBT staff felt personally discriminated against and that their sexuality had 'resulted in severe levels of discrimination by students, but also surprisingly colleagues as well'.

Why do homophobic attitudes continue?

There is an increasing acceptance in society of diversity of all kinds, but lingering and covert prejudices and attitudes remain in relation to all outgroups, despite legislation protecting the rights of individuals on the basis of age, gender, ethnicity, religion, disability and sexual orientation. In the case of sexuality, the declared intentions of the state to respect the rights of minorities may exist alongside homophobic attitudes when religion is in conflict with these aims. This dilemma will be considered further in Chapter 10. A particular case is that of Ireland, where research indicates both that schools are unwilling to look at LGBT issues in sex education and that there are 'significant levels of homophobic bullying in schools and a limited response from teachers and by extension from school management', because of the power of the Church (McNamara and Norman, 2010: 545). Similarly, a review of practice in one region of Ireland shows that in relation to homosexuality, a 'widespread culture of related mockery and abuse is allowed to go largely unchallenged' (Morrison and Lumby, 2006: 36). Teachers are tolerating homophobic attitudes at least in part because their own Catholic backgrounds lead them to want to deter gayness. In such a situation, attempting to bring about equality through policy and legislation will not be sufficient. To ensure equality, it is necessary to make positive moves to accept difference in sexuality.

Conflict between the attitudes of the state and religion may also occur in Muslim schools, although the Association of Muslim Schools (2015) states that it is against homophobia. Nevertheless, in some Muslim countries and communities homosexuality is illegal, and likely to attract, at the least, moral disapproval and, at worst, severe punishment. Where religious values are in conflict with a culture of respect and equality for all, it will be necessary to take a stance that prioritizes equity and equality for all members of the community (see Chapter 10).

We live in a changing culture where there is increasing sensitivity about the rights of minorities. Some older people may not be in touch with the norms of the present day, or a combination of apathy and ignorance may mean that people of any age do not speak out against homophobia. In particular, changes in the use of discriminatory language may be slow to register, and younger children may not understand how use of the word 'gay' might be offensive. However, ethnographic research with boys from three sixth forms found that in their schools the majority supported gay rights, and that gay students did not experience bullying or the use of homophobic language (McCormack, 2011). It appears that, at least in some age groups and circumstances, being tolerant and accepting difference can become the norm.

Policy and practice to counter homophobia

In our two case examples in this chapter the senior staff have worked to ensure that all those associated with the school community share the same values, establishing an ethos of inclusion and cultural justice. For example, at Winburg School part of the recruitment strategy is to ask all potential staff their views 'about things like sexuality'. The head stated: 'We want to employ people who hold our values'. Some of the ways in which such an ethos can be encouraged are through the curriculum, through professional development, through working with parents and the wider community, and through the development and maintenance of a formal policy.

The curriculum

In the secondary school example, change had come about particularly through personal, social and health education (PSHE) and the humanities, although links were made across other aspects of the curriculum:

Winburg: curriculum

One of the key things is joining up every aspect of the school's work and not just looking at sexuality in isolation. For example, look at the link with citizenship, with English and with science, with all the subjects. Look at how the curriculum works to develop values across the board. Make sure that you are adapting the curriculum to changing circumstances. For example, discovery of lack of clarity about transgender issues in Years 10 and 11 and amongst some staff led to further work with Stonewall who suggested another organization who sent in speakers.

Staff felt there was not enough time to talk about sexuality so we took a day out and looked at equality issues and had speakers come in. That day formed the basis of coursework for their humanities GCSE.

A growing challenge is the development of online issues in relation to bullying of all kinds, including homophobic bullying. The head at Winburg School commented that although the school focuses on online issues in their Values and Ethics (PSHE) course, 'whatever we do we are ten paces behind' and that parents are also faced with the same difficulty. Cyber-bullying is particularly difficult to monitor because of the speed of development and the fact that it is not limited by time or place.

At Glentanna School the impact of sexuality on the curriculum extended to core subjects when a probationer teacher chose to run a project around the book *Bill's New Frock*:

Glentanna: curriculum

She questioned the children before they read it asking what they thought about words like 'boy', 'girl', 'pink'. Did they see them as positive or negative? Once they had read the book she gave them the same questions again and they were much more positive afterwards. Now we have implemented study of the book in Primary 5 (English Year 4). What happened was not planned but it had an impact.

Professional development

In Glentanna School, professional development was vital in following up the initial impetus to change:

Glentanna: professional development

It just happened that the local authority had training at that time that was about that very thing and I went along. As it turned out a couple of colleagues from the school were there too. They had gone independently, but it meant that there were three of us from the school and that was useful. The training was run by Stonewall, who also provided resources. When we went back to school, the head was really positive and wanted to take it forward. We joined Stonewall as a school, and that gave us access to more materials.

The inclusion of a learning assistant undergoing further training was felt to be of key importance, because of the need for enlightened lunchtime supervision at that time of day, when it is most likely that homophobic language will be used. In Winburg School the head commented: 'It is important to build capacity within the organization itself. In the early days we relied a lot on outside agencies. I think it is OK to do that at the start and then to work towards staff training staff and students working with students'. Further development involved working with other stakeholders, including parents.

Working with parents and the wider community

Links with parents and the wider community were forged in both the case example schools:

Glentanna: working with parents

A big part of taking things forward was parents' night, where we had an information desk that the children ran. It had posters for display around the school and booklets for background information for the teachers and the parents were able to see what we were doing. We had a comments box for the parents and all the comments relating to diversity were positive.

Also the parents' night event was good as we really reached a lot of parents. The parents always come to parents' night and everyone saw the resources and lots of them stopped at the stall and took time. When you send letters home about something new they get lost. When we have a curricular night not many parents come, maybe 10 per cent, but 95 per cent come to parents' night so it was a good way of involving parents. I would definitely recommend that.

The children's involvement has also been a driver. Some of the older children wrote to the Director of Education saying that all schools should be Stonewall schools. He came and he was pleased and impressed by the children and there was talk of rolling the programme out to all schools with a great deal of enthusiasm from the authority.

In Winburg School, the head teacher was aware of the importance of governors being involved and committed to a policy on sexuality: 'I had a good chair of governors and not all governing bodies are that supportive. I have not heard many governing bodies talking seriously about equality'.

Developing and maintaining policy

At Winburg School there has been a slow, steady development of a policy that has then influenced practice:

Winburg: developing policy

We started with a working group of staff and talked a lot about how the policy would fit. We then worked with some students and with outside agencies including Stonewall and the local authority. We also looked at good practice from other schools. It took a year in all to develop.

In Glentanna School, in contrast, changes in practice were followed by the development of a written policy:

Glentanna: developing policy

Once we finalize the policy we will share it amongst everyone. The work is here, but we are now putting the policy into writing. In our case practice has preceded written policy. If you have good practice, the policy will follow. We made sure that everyone was included in the consultation, including the children.

Embedding inclusive attitudes to sexuality in the two schools also involved having a clear action plan attached to the policy, ensuring that it is monitored and reviewed to maintain it at the forefront of the school's values:

Winburg: monitoring progress

We need to monitor at different levels, staff, students and survey with parents. However, you can monitor anything to death. What is important is the impact which is not always measurable – it is about ethos and harmony, and you can sense it when you go round the school.

Glentanna: maintaining the initiative

We have now established this initiative and the current group of children know what the deal is. The challenge now is keeping it to the forefront, keeping everyone up to date and informed.

There is evidence of good policy and practice feeding through into the culture and daily life of these two schools, but there is a continuing challenge, identified earlier in the chapter, which involves a change of mindset. This involves heteronormativity not being the taken-for-granted norm and the school being proactive in its stance on sexuality. This needs to be continually demonstrated throughout the curriculum, including within the sex education curriculum. There is also the ongoing challenge of cyber-bullying – the use of texts, emails and social networks as a form of bullying that is potentially homophobic.

Leadership in schools bringing about a more inclusive culture

The experience of the two case example schools exemplifies positive actions to counter homophobia and to celebrate difference, and the importance of working with parents and governors, as well as students and staff. All of these coincide with suggestions from official guidance and research into what constitutes good practice. Ofsted (2012) refers to developing a culture of mutual respect, with the school having a clear set of inclusive values that are modelled by staff 'in their interactions with each other, with parents and carers, and with pupils' (2012: 8). There is, of course, more specific and detailed advice relating to addressing homophobic attitudes available from Stonewall and, for example, DCSF (2007) or Jennett (2004).

In addition, Ofsted (2012) places the onus for evaluating the effectiveness of the leadership's actions in relation to a school's culture on the governing body, and indicates the importance of including anti-bullying in initial teacher education. Ellis with High (2004: 224) go further to suggest that pre-service and in-service courses should make teachers look at their values and practice, to be proactive rather than just reactive. Warwick et al. (2004) stress the need to draw on the expertise of outside groups and agencies, and advocate the promotion of research and knowledge in the area, suggesting that teachers work together to develop and share successful curricular initiatives. This is particularly because, according to the Teacher Support Network (2014), a majority of teachers do not yet feel comfortable to teach about same-sex marriage and LGBT-related issues.

Establishing sexual identity is a key part of the maturation process, when all young people are likely to feel sensitive and vulnerable as they change and develop. If young people identify as LGBT or if they are questioning their identity, they may be especially vulnerable and open to potential bullying by peers and adults. Schools can do much to establish a culture where all individuals are valued and difference is something to be accepted or celebrated rather than ridiculed. Leaders at all levels in schools play an important part in ensuring that values are examined and norms are questioned.

Key actions

- Involve all members of the school community.
- Identify and discuss homophobic language.
- Eradicate homophobic bullying.
- Move beyond a culture of heteronormativity.
- Make use of opportunities across the curriculum to discuss sexuality.
- Work towards a policy for your school.

For reflection and discussion

If you were able to carry out an audit of heteronormative assumptions in the curriculum of your school, what might you discover? What steps might you take as a result?

Additional reading

For information about useful resources for teaching around sexuality:

Stonewall website, www.stonewall.org.uk/our-work/education-resources (accessed 10.05.16).

For guidance on safeguarding:

DCFS (2007) *Homophobic Bullying: Safe to Learn – Embedding Anti-Bullying Work in Schools.* Nottingham: DCSF.
DfE (2014) *Keeping Children Safe in Education: Statutory Guidance for Schools and Colleges.* www.gov.uk/government/uploads/system/uploads/attachment_data/file/447595/KCSIE_July_2015.pdf (accessed 05.05.16).

For further consideration of the wider implications of sexuality for school leaders:

Myers, K. (2002) 'Dilemmas of leadership: sexuality and schools', *International Journal of Leadership in Education*, 5 (4): 285–302.

For a more theoretical discussion of out-groups:

Lumby, J. with Coleman, M. (2007) *Leadership and Diversity: Challenging Theory and Practice in Education.* London: Sage. Chapter 3.

For a more theoretical approach to sexuality, sex and gender:

Youdell, D. (2005) 'Sex-gender-sexuality: how sex, gender and sexuality constellations are constituted in secondary schools', *Gender and Education*, 17 (3): 249–70.

9

Ethnicity and equality

Ethnicity remains a key area of potential inequality in the education system. Although intersecting with other facets of possible inequality, for example socioeconomic class, religion and gender, ethnicity itself is a focus for racism, discrimination, bullying and low expectations, all of which impact on accessing educational opportunities. Increasing levels of migration into and within Europe have put a fresh emphasis on ethnicity as a factor in schools and in society more generally. In the context of a growing ethnic minority population, schools may need to continually re-assess their practice to ensure that they are offering the best possible educational experience to all.

In this chapter we ask you to think about:

- ethnicity and the school population in England
- the intersectionality of ethnicity, particularly with socioeconomic status
- racism, perceptions and mindsets
- taking a cultural or recognition approach to ethnicity in schools.

We are using the term 'ethnicity' rather than the term 'race', although we still talk about 'racism' when considering discrimination relating to ethnicity. In this chapter we focus on issues of racism that affect all ethnic minorities. There are, of course, issues relating to particular ethnic groups, and though the chapter includes a few specific references and examples, we do not have sufficient space to give full consideration to every major community.

The term 'ethnicity' is tricky, as it comprises two elements: culture – including language, dress and customs – and skin colour. Which of these two aspects is seen as more important varies in time and place. The relationship between the two is complex, as people of different colour may share the same culture, whilst people with different cultures might be White (Crozier, 2014). In the latter case, Whiteness does not necessarily protect a group from racist attitudes. For example, Roma, Travellers and Gypsies, as well as the recent influxes of Eastern European people into Western Europe, experience racist discrimination and stereotyping, and anti-semitism continues across Europe. The term 'Black and Minority Ethnic' (BME) is commonly used in the UK to include anyone who is not White British, but this term is open to challenge as it prioritizes White as the norm. An alternative term, 'Black and Global Majority' (BGM) has been proposed (Campbell-Stephens, 2009) and is a more accurate representation of the world population, but here we use the more commonly accepted term BME.

In this chapter we draw on illustrative case examples from four co-educational schools: Allenridge (11–18) and Maclear (11–16) community schools, both in the south of England; and Tulback Academy (11–18) and Trichard Community Infants, both in inner London.

The context: ethnicity, intersectionality and the school population in England

The proportion of students in English schools who are from a BME background is steadily rising. In 2012, for example, 27.6 per cent of primary school pupils were BME and by 2015 this figure had risen to 30.4 per cent. In secondary schools comparative figures were 23.2 per cent rising to 26.6 per cent (DfE, 2013, 2015c). These are the average figures, and of course the rise is not evenly spread across the country but varies between regions, and between urban and rural locations. For example, 81 per cent of pupils in inner London boroughs are from BME backgrounds, in contrast to 11 per cent in the North-East of England (Coughlan, 2015). The proportion of BME students in other UK countries is less than in England. For example, figures for Wales (Lewis and Starkey, 2013) indicate that 93 per cent of students are White, although the proportion of BME students is growing.

Just as there is widespread concern about the gender attainment gap (see Chapter 7), there is concern about attainment gaps between the various ethnic groups, for example the poor academic attainment of White students from disadvantaged socioeconomic backgrounds. In general, all groups in England have improved in terms of five good A–C grades at GCSE between 2004 and 2013 (Strand, 2015). It is also good news that gaps in educational attainment between White British and other ethnic groups have narrowed quite dramatically, although some differences between ethnic groups still remain. A group where school attendance and attainment is particularly low is the Roma, Traveller and Gypsy communities (Wilkin et al., 2010), and this is true throughout Europe (Szalai, 2011). The importance of monitoring student data has been explored in other chapters, and it remains one of the main tools in relation to ensuring equality for BME children. The head of Allenridge School commented: 'We cut the data on the protected characteristics – including gender, class (FSM) [free school meals], ethnicity, and different types of special needs – in many ways and monitor the gaps closely'.

It is important for schools to monitor the progress of their various ethnic groups, yet to take an intersectionality approach may be more meaningful. The intersection of ethnicity and religion is considered more fully in Chapter 10, and the intersection of ethnicity with migration in Chapter 11. Here we look briefly at the intersection of ethnicity and socioeconomic status. As we have seen throughout the book, those who start with more tend to prosper, and socioeconomic status is strongly linked to academic success. Eligibility for free school meals is a common indicator of relative poverty and it is apparent that some groups of ethnic minority students on FSM achieve more than others. For example, as indicated above, White students on FSM achieve less than any other group.

Stokes et al. (2015) found that the important factors in the relative success of BME students on FSM are the attitudes of parents, the resilience of the students and the impact of schools. Parental aspirations of most BME pupils tend to be high, and when parents have high aspirations they are often more involved with their children's education. Social capital plays an important part in the differential achievement of children from varied socioeconomic backgrounds and ethnic groups. Parents of children from some minority ethnic groups are likely to arrange for their children to attend supplementary schools, whereas White British children from a poor socioeconomic background are less likely to do so. The attitude of students is important, and positive and resilient attitudes appear to be more common in children from BME than from White British backgrounds. In contrast, risk factors for poor achievement, including not completing homework, truancy and exclusion, tend to be more prevalent in White British communities. The school factors that are most strongly related to raising the achievement of BME students with poorer economic circumstances are: an inclusive ethos; high expectations; monitoring and tracking students; and effective classroom practices. It is a challenge for schools to try to implement these rather general, although laudable, aims and make them a reality.

Despite the very positive progress of most ethnic minorities in levels of educational achievement, there are many ways in which ethnicity may negatively impact on students, particularly through pervasive racist attitudes.

Racism, perceptions and mindsets

Despite the best intentions of leaders in schools, there are likely to be racist incidents and examples of racist stereotyping amongst staff and students. In the following example, the deputy head of Tulback School outlined a problem not with the student body but with ancillary staff, potentially impacting on the ethos of the school:

Tulback: dealing with overt racism

We had a real issue with racism in the canteen. There were two groups within the staff, one White and one Black, and there was some fairly unprofessional behaviour sparked off by an incident that showed there were some entrenched racist views. I searched for training to tackle it head on and brought in trainers because of the sensitivity of the issue to explore attitudes safely. They did come in and staff spoke highly of it. It seemed that staff did not understand that what they were doing was racist, so initially it seemed successful but long term it has had limited impact. The outcome is that they stopped using racist language but entrenched views like that are very hard to change. We will have to look to do something different next year.

Overt racism, as in this example, must be addressed – yet racism is often covert or even unconscious, with ethnicity impacting on perceptions, aspirations and identity in subtle ways. This leads to anomalies in the identification of special needs, rates of exclusion and access to types of higher education throughout Europe (European Agency for Development in Special Needs Education, 2009). In England Black Caribbean, and Mixed Black and White Caribbean students, are particularly likely to be identified as having social and emotional difficulties, and are twice as likely as White British students to be excluded, whilst rates of exclusion for Indian and Chinese students are very low (Strand, 2015). Also, most BME students tend to progress to the less prestigious higher education institutions and be limited to particular subject areas, and are less likely to achieve a good degree than their White counterparts (Stevenson, 2012).

In the following example, the head teacher is implicitly aware of the underlying assumptions of and about pupils, fuelled by the concept of Whiteness and the importance of social capital that is part of being White – or at least, White and middle class:

Allenridge: measuring against Whiteness and expectations of ethnic minority students

In my view, the main barriers to learning that we deal with are the ones that the students bring with them. They have their own blind spots or perceptions of their own worth and ambitions. We spend a lot of time convincing them of their abilities and encouraging them to be ambitious.

We are a 55 per cent ethnic minority school and our main feeder school is 85 per cent. They [the students entering the secondary school] exist in something of a linguistically underdeveloped enclave. The children are bright, bubbly and exuberant and when they arrive they are full of themselves. But they then meet articulate, middle-class White children for the first time and for a while it smashes them to pieces. It makes them go quiet and many have reported that they felt stupid for some time. It takes us a while to convince them that they are just as clever as the more articulate kids.

It is difficult to amend expectations, and the head teacher went on to outline how he had followed up the children from the feeder school he mentioned to see which degree courses they subsequently enrolled on. Their choices did not include English, History, Geography or Modern Languages, although there was a good range of technical and more vocational subjects. It appears that the expectations of the students and possibly their teachers had been framed by stereotypes of traditional subject choices and potential career routes for BME students.

We live in a society where there are some taken-for-granted assumptions, deeply ingrained in most people's ways of thinking, that fuel expectations and stereotypes about individuals according to their ethnicity. The most striking example is that teachers tend to under-estimate the ability of Black children and are likely to have high expectations of Chinese children, who are stereotyped as hard-working and able (Archer and Francis, 2007). It is interesting that implicit judgements are made that White is the baseline against which every other ethnicity is judged. Critical Race Theory has contributed to the understanding that Whiteness is assumed to be the norm, which tends to privilege those who are White, unintentionally discriminating against those who are 'other' in terms of Whiteness. This can be described as institutional racism, famously defined in the Macpherson report on the Stephen Lawrence murder as:

> The collective failure of an organisation to provide an appropriate and professional service to people because of their colour, culture or ethnic origin. It can be seen or detected in processes, attitudes and behaviour which amount to discrimination through unwitting prejudice, ignorance, thoughtlessness and racist stereotyping which disadvantage minority ethnic people. (Macpherson, 1999: para. 6.34)

The subtlety of institutional racism is best illustrated by small incidents that, individually, might be seen as unimportant and are therefore rarely reported.

Critical Race Theory endorses the idea of individual stories to expose just how subtle and endemic racism can be in society. An example is quoted by Bradbury (2014: 26) of Abeje, an African-Caribbean 5-year-old girl who was 'hard-working, vocal and keen to engage with the range of activities on offer'. However, her confidence and enthusiasm were interpreted as being resistant to rules, and she was seen as 'deviant and aggressive' and a 'diva'. Her appearance – she wore an Afro and a Rasa hat – emphasized her difference in the classroom. The importance of appearance has been analysed by Youdell (2004), who identifies how the physical presentation – the slouching and manner of walking – of young Black male students is interpreted by the school in ways that stigmatize the students. The influence of stereotypes can also be seen, for example, in assumptions about Chinese girls (Mau, 2014: 123) who might feel uncomfortable with being singled out to 'perform their Chineseness', and are then categorized as being shy and quiet, the usual stereotype applied to Chinese girls. Such requests may be well intentioned, but have the effect of exoticizing and 'othering' them.

Ethnic stereotypes relating to students are powerful and affect the way that they are perceived in the classroom, idealizing some and demonizing others, affecting the level of teacher expectations. This then impacts on their performance and achievement. Taking into account the subtle effects of underlying attitudes to ethnicity, we would endorse schools taking a recognition or cultural approach, as discussed in Chapter 5, to ethnic minority communities.

Taking a recognition or cultural approach in school

Where there are marginalized groups it is appropriate for leaders to take a cultural or recognition approach, as discussed in Chapters 1 and 5, so that such groups are more strongly acknowledged and supported. This is a mainstreaming approach and it impacts on all the underlying structures of the school. Here we focus on the curriculum, relationships with parents and the local community, and the overall ethos of the school.

The curriculum

Schools are faced with providing a curriculum that honours the different cultures represented by the student body whilst ensuring that they provide their pupils with the same opportunities as those of White middle-class pupils when it comes to accessing higher education and careers. In this, they may be hampered by the narrowness of the imposed curriculum. In England the curriculum is largely content-driven, which means it is likely to have 'implicit values' (Elton-Chalcraft, 2009: 3) that make it harder for teachers to reflect on the nature of what is being taught and its effects on those from different cultures and backgrounds. Implicit values are also built into the assessment system. For example, the knowledge and understanding of children with a second language are not taken into account in testing the literacy skills of young children. Moreover, the stress on numeracy and literacy in primary schools, and in England on achieving good GCSE grades in secondary schools, tends to 'crowd out' the study of citizenship, PSHE and religious education, where questions relating to ethnicity and racism might be most easily addressed. The head of Allenridge School commented on the way in which the school's curriculum is constrained and on the values that it seeks to uphold:

> We have created a family here and we stimulate the students as much as we can within the constraints of the National Curriculum, National Targets and Ofsted readiness. We are guided throughout by principles of natural justice, fairness and people being treated equally.

There are the issues of the hidden curriculum, for example whether teachers are fair in the way that they choose children to answer in class, the ways in which play-times and lunchtimes are organized, the types of uniform available and the nature of the displays and school-related literature, including the prospectus. All may unconsciously relate to a White middle-class norm.

Language may be a particular barrier to accessing the curriculum, especially for children new to the country or to a school where English (or Welsh) is not the language spoken in the home. It may be necessary to ensure that there is quite focused language support, and this is considered further in Chapter 11 on migrant children.

Reaching out to parents and the local community

Trichard: reaching out to parents

I heard one of the governors say in a meeting, 'schools are not just for children – they are for parents as well'. It made me think. That shift is where this school has ground to make up. I think crossing [ethnic] boundaries works better with children in school than it does with parents in the school community.

It is no good looking at parents separately. What joins them is their wanting the best for their children. I have always felt that creating a focus around the children's learning is the way to join communities up and we are working on a new parental engagement plan again to try and get parental involvement in school to gel.

The laudable intentions in the example above may be the key to building relationships with parents from various ethnic communities. As we have seen, parents of BME children are often particularly aspirational and interested in their children's education (Stokes et al., 2015). However, this does not necessarily mean that the school and the parents are fully sympathetic to each other, for example when parents have experienced racism in their own schooling or feel that cultural stereotypes are being reinforced by the school. A study of relationships between Black parents and schools found that power relations were crucial, and that parents wanted to know that they could trust schools to realize their children's full potential and be free of racial bias (Cork, 2005). Perceptions of families from Traveller, Gypsy and Roma communities tend to be that their children are bullied and therefore not safe at school, that what they are taught at school is not necessarily relevant to them and that their culture is not

respected (D'Arcy, 2014). There is obviously conflict between the expectations of schools with regard to students from this community and how the
community perceives the education that is being offered. Chinese parents
tend to be critical of the British school system, despite a perception on
the part of teachers that they are extremely pleased with their children's
education (Archer and Francis, 2007). It seems likely that, at least on occa-
sion, teachers and parents from ethnic minorities are 'on parallel tracks
not actually hearing each other' (2007: 72).

In the example that follows, there is evidence of a school building relationships with parents through the good experience of their children, but
the message is that this type of trust will take time:

Maclear: building relationships with parents

But at parents' evening there are still instances where our students are
the translators for their parents and it's interesting. The Somali community is significant here. I think they're second and third generation
and my understanding is they came in to London and then there was a
wave that then moved on, so there was a familiarity with British culture
and language and I think certainly when I arrived, when I used to get ...
it was to do with child protection issues, one or two. I used to get
deputations, groups of parents that come in and try and shout at me
to tell me how to do things. But we've moved a long way from that.
Primarily I think it's the students, because it's the students who are
completely on side and are happy and doing well and so the parents ...
all of that drops away and our attendance at parents' evenings ... A lot
of parents live right down in the city and transport in this city, like many
others, is not easy or straightforward. We get between 60 per cent and
70 per cent which is much higher than it's been. I mean we've been
watching it go up, it's amazing, I think.

School ethos

Relationships in school, and between a school and the community, are
dependent on sharing values within the school that underpin the attitudes
and expectations of staff. In the following example the inclusive ethos that
has been achieved in the school is supported by staff undertaking formal
diversity training when they first arrive:

Allenridge: staff expectations and training

We are a multi-ethnic and multi-class school, and teachers don't come here unless they embrace that fact ... There are over 50 languages spoken in the school. We celebrate other cultures and tell people's stories ... In terms of organization the most important thing is to provide a secure space policed with a strong sense of justice. I don't necessarily set great store by interventions such as anti-racist programmes; they can be counter-productive. It is most important that children and staff feel safe, loved and stimulated.

We have a workbook on embracing diversity that all new staff work through. At the end they take a test and get a certificate. You see the certificates up on the walls of some offices and classrooms. It gives staff a good grounding in the law related to protected characteristics.

In this school, the ethos and the focused professional development are both vital in helping staff to challenge cultures of White privilege and automatic White dominance. At the same time they encourage social cohesion amongst different groups (Elton-Chalcraft, 2009).

A recognition approach would also include recognizing the importance and potential of BME staff, not only in terms of their equitable treatment but also in helping to provide role models of BME leaders for students. Having looked at the proportion of BME staff in leadership positions, Allenridge School ran a leadership development course primarily for BME staff, to encourage and support them in looking for promotion. In Tulback School there is awareness of the importance of role modelling through its leadership team:

Allenridge: diversity and leadership

At this school about 25 per cent of the staff are from ethnic minorities and there is very much a feeling of being a multicultural staff team. You always have to ask yourself the question, 'Are you guilty of unconscious bias?' There is a frightening possibility that you are biased unconsciously but we have developed a family here where I believe all minority ethnic staff and students feel empowered to aspire.

Tulback: diversity and role modelling

It is quite a diverse leadership team and we do our best to model strong decision making from a cohesive co-operative base. The team represents the diversity of the student population. Systems support diversity and equality, for example promoting equality of opportunity for staff ... We are also very aware in terms of our appointments; we are very aware of the relevant legislation and of being very open minded, e.g. about age and ethnicity.

At the end of this chapter are recommendations for further reading relating to potential discrimination against BME staff in accessing leadership positions.

An inclusive ethos honouring ethnic and other types of diversity is essential to ensure equality for all, as well as ensuring a safe environment where students are not bullied and devalued. Overall, it is important to look critically at the values that underpin the day-to-day actions within the school and at how they are actually being applied. Values and moral purpose in schools are of paramount importance in taking a cultural approach. Campbell-Stephens states:

> I think the way that you judge which kind of moral purpose underpins most systems is to view who benefits and who does not, what they choose to measure, what they choose to reward and affirm and what the outcomes are for the masses who go through that process. (Campbell-Stephens, 2009: 19)

Combating racism and working towards equality in relation to ethnicity will require a critical examination of all aspects of school life, questioning taken-for-granted attitudes and assumptions.

Key actions

To work towards equity and equality for all students, irrespective of ethnicity, leaders in schools should:

- Encourage a mindset of high expectations for all amongst staff and students.
- Examine the overt and hidden curriculum to ensure that Whiteness is not the norm against which everything else is measured.

- Provide support for staff in relation to diversity, including leadership development for BME staff.
- Reach out to parents and the local community to involve them in the work and ethos of the school.

For reflection and discussion

Taking the Campbell-Stephens quotation above, interrogate the situation in your school with regard to ethnicity, asking:

- Who benefits and who does not?
- What are you measuring?
- What are you choosing to reward and affirm?
- What are the outcomes for all the groups of students in the school?

Additional reading

For succinct introductions to Critical Race Theory:

Gillborn, D. (undated) *Critical Race Theory and Education: Racism and Antiracism in Educational Theory and Praxis.* http://eprints.ioe.ac.uk/1661/1/Gillborn2006 critical11.pdf (accessed 08.05.16).

Rollock, N. and Gillborn, D. (2011) *Critical Race Theory.* BERA. www.bera.ac.uk/ wp-content/uploads/2014/03/Critical-Race-Theory-CRT-.pdf?noredirect=1 (accessed 08.05.16).

A detailed analysis of pupil achievement, ethnicity and deprivation may be found in:

Strand, S. (2015) *Ethnicity, Deprivation and Educational Achievement at Age 16 in England: Trends Over Time.* Annex to compendium of evidence on ethnic minority resilience to the effects of deprivation on attainment. London: DfE.

For further reading on Traveller and Roma communities:

Wilkin, A., Derrington, C., White, R., Martin, R., Foster, B., Kinder, K. and Rutt, S. (2010) *Improving the Outcomes for Gypsy, Roma and Traveller Pupils: Final Report.* London: DfE.

The barriers to BME leadership and possible ways forward are discussed in:

Bush, T., Glover, D. and Sood, K. (2006) 'Black and Minority Ethnic leaders in England: a portrait', *School Leadership and Management*, 26 (3): 289–305.

Coleman, M. and Campbell-Stephens, R. (2010) 'Perceptions of career progress: the experience of Black and Minority Ethnic school leaders', *School Leadership and Management*, 30 (1): 35–49.

10

Religion and equality

Schools in the UK have been subject to regulation concerning religious worship and religious education since early in the twentieth century. The current framework was essentially established in the 1940s. As society becomes more diverse, and the nature of religious belief and practice evolves, questions have been raised about the future of religion in schools, which query how fit for purpose are requirements such as a daily act of worship or public funding of faith schools. Some argue that the place of religion in education reflects outdated attitudes and is in urgent need of transformation (Dinham and Shaw, 2015). Terrorists linking their acts to religion, and the radicalization of a small number of children, have further sharpened the focus on religion in schools.

In this context of uncertainty and anxiety, we focus on how religion and equality might be understood in all schools, both faith and community. Faith schools are those with a religious character that often take account of religion in their entry criteria. Schools that do not specifically have a religious character are referred to in this chapter as community schools.

Striving for equality in relation to religion is different from other aspects of equality in one important respect: those of a particular faith may believe that how to act is directed by a spiritual source, such as the Bible or the *Qur'an*. For believers, such religious texts have an authority that may overrule social or legal codes. The interpretation of texts may bring them into conflict with aspects of equality in areas such as gender or sexuality. When fundamental convictions are involved, compromise and tolerance are easy to stipulate but may be less easy to achieve.

A religion might also be associated with a particular ethnic group, and so believers may be subject to racist stereotypes. Consequently, discussion of equality and religion in schools must take account of the racism and sexism that sometimes influence attitudes and debate. An intersectionality approach, as discussed in Chapter 3, taking account of religion and also other characteristics, is necessary for all who attempt to understand how religious equality might be enacted in schools.

In this chapter we ask you to think about:

- the context for religious equality in schools
- how we might understand religious equality
- differing approaches to achieving greater religious equality, including:

  o values
  o religious education
  o intercultural education.

Case examples are drawn from three schools: St Mary's Catholic School (11–16) in the south of England; Rawabit Islamic School (5–11) in London; and Maclear Community School (11–16) in the south of England. All are co-educational.

The context for religion and equality

Media attention on declining church attendance has created the impression that the role of religion in society is waning. This oversimplifies a process of complex change. Modood and Calhoun (2015) point out that one in five nations in Europe has a state religion and that every state gives funding to faith schools. In terms of personal religious belief, only 25 per cent in the 2011 UK Census stated that they were not affiliated to any religion, and in a 2015 online survey by YouGov, 51 per cent of adults identified themselves as Christian, with the percentage even higher, at 69 per cent, for over 55s. Davie (2009) suggests that though attendance at church may be declining amongst Christians in the UK, the majority of the population still feel connected to a faith. Others, though not affiliated to a religion, may feel deeply committed to a belief system such as humanism.

Change is in part a result of migration. For example, the number of Polish people arriving in the UK has increased Catholic worship (Rienzo and Vargas-Silva, 2014). Throughout the UK and Europe, the diaspora from many parts of the world has also increased the range of religions and sects. An overview of the UK is provided in Table 10.1.

Table 10.1   Religion in the home countries, UK

Religion	% England & Wales	% Scotland	% Northern Ireland
Christian	72	65	86
Muslim	3	1.4	1.0
Hindu	1	>0.1	>0.1
Sikh	0.8	>0.1	2.0
Buddhist	1.0	>0.1	>0.1
Jewish	1.0	>0.1	>0.1
Other religions	1.0		
No religious affiliation	15	28	14
Chose not to answer	8	5	

Source: Francis et al. (2015: 250)

Overall, Modood and Calhoun (2015) predict that in ten years' time one in eight of those reaching adulthood in the UK will be of a minority faith, with the proportion higher in some areas where there is geographic clustering.

Religion and policy

Recent events have amplified the focus on religion in schools. Terrorist acts in Europe and the radicalization of some pupils have increased the urgency and importance of appropriate religious and spiritual education. In Paris in 2015 a declaration by European education ministers responded to deep concern about extremism by emphasizing the vital role of schools in cultivating common values, critical understanding, tolerance of others, and abhorrence of all forms of racism and discrimination (European Union, 2015b).

The response in terms of education policy and practice has varied. There is ongoing debate about the place of faith schools and the degree to which they contribute to or undermine social cohesion. Despite some public opposition, both the number and range of faith schools have increased. Thirty-five per cent of maintained schools in England are faith schools (Allen and West, 2011), the large majority of which (98 per cent) are Church of England or Roman Catholic. Fifty-eight schools reflect a different religion: 'Jewish (38); Muslim (11); Sikh (4); Greek Orthodox, Hindu, Quaker, Seventh Day Adventist, United Reform Church (1 each)' (Allen and West, 2011: 693).

Faith schools offer the possibility of protecting not only the religion itself but also the culture and identity of a community through religion (Patrikios and Curtice, 2014). This positive perspective is countered by a range of anxieties about the effect of religious segregation. In England, the so-called 'Trojan horse investigation' of the suspected inappropriate imposition of narrow Islamic values in several schools in Birmingham (Clarke, 2014) 'agitated many, alienated others and left pedagogical and social scars' (Panjwani, 2014: 9). In Northern Ireland, segregation into Protestant and Catholic schools continues to raise concerns (Hughes, 2011).

The role of faith schools has become entwined in debates not only about religious segregation but also about socioeconomic segregation in a marketized education environment. There is evidence that faith schools' enrolment is manipulated by the middle class to achieve socioeconomic segregation in favour of those from privileged economic backgrounds. Allen and West (2011: 707) found that 'children of higher social class, higher parental education and higher income households are more likely to attend faith schools' and that parents who had received a higher education were more likely to pick up the clues in the admissions criteria about successful entry than parents who were of the same religion but had not. The Sutton Trust (2013) suggested that faith schools were over-represented amongst the most socially selective schools in England. Yet many families wish for a faith-based education, and such demand is growing. *The Guardian* (Abrams, 2011) reported that an Islamic School had 1,500 applications for just 60 places. The growth in unregulated faith-based Islamic and Jewish schools has raised concerns (Walker, 2015), but is evidence of the strong demand for faith-based education.

Given the level of Islamophobia (van Driel, 2004), anti-semitism (National Union of Teachers, n.d.) and sectarianism amongst Christians (Flint, 2007), both faith and community schools must find ways of nurturing what is valued in religion and protecting children from discrimination on the grounds of their faith (Ossewaarde, 2014; Parker-Jenkins, 2014). They also need to educate children to understand that, for example, Christian, Muslim or Jewish people cannot be seen as homogeneous groups associated with a particular ethnicity or a single set of religious beliefs.

Staff, too, are subject to discrimination. Those overtly identifying with a religion can be subject to suspicion and a negative assessment of their capability. Shah and Shaikh (2010) found male Muslim teachers afraid to network for fear of being tagged as extremist. They are also less likely to be promoted. Sandberg (2011) refers to the discrimination evident in Protestant attitudes to Catholic teachers, and vice versa, in sectarian Northern Ireland and Scotland. Not only are individual members of staff disadvantaged, but also children, through witnessing inappropriate attitudes to minority-religion staff.

Balancing such negative concerns is a persistent conviction of the importance of religion in education. In England, the 2015 YouGov survey quoted above found a large majority of adults, 77 per cent, believe that religious education should be part of the compulsory national curriculum. Children, too, value religion. A survey of 13- to 15-year-old girls generated two key findings (Francis et al., 2015). First, more children believe religion is a force for good in the world than the opposite. However, an exception is in relation to Islam, where views were more negative and influenced by the child's religious affiliation. Though an equal number of active Christians believed that Islam was a force for good and a force for harm in the world, a greater proportion of those who did not have a religion, or only a nominal religion, believed Islam to be more a force for harm.

Attitudes that are both misinformed and antagonistic towards Muslims have come to be termed, in shorthand, 'Islamophobia'. Although targeted at people of the faith of Islam, hostile attitudes are often based on racist stereotypes that turn Muslim pupils into 'other'. Both Muslim boys and girls experience discrimination on the grounds of religion and race, as inextricably entwined. Actual violence against Muslim pupils is rare, but instances of verbal abuse and aggression are growing (Vryonides, 2014). Muslim boys, in particular, feel stigmatized by being associated with terrorism (Shain, 2011). The requirement for teachers in British schools to be alert to and report any suspicion of extremism as part of the government's Prevent strategy is feared by some to have exacerbated Islamophobia in schools and places teachers in a difficult position (Sian, 2015). Many schools have responded with much energy, focusing on a positive agenda of building social cohesion as the primary objective, rather than the negative objective of preventing radicalization and terrorism (Phillips et al., 2011).

The second finding of particular relevance from the Francis et al. (2015) survey is that studying religion at school is a significant force in shaping young people's views about religion, more so than their family, the Internet or television. It would seem that the public, children themselves and European education ministers all agree that religion has a vital place in schools. This is not just in terms of educating pupils about the spiritual, cultural and artistic riches of religions, and supporting them to practise a faith if they wish, but also in positioning positive attitudes to diverse religions as part of what it means to be a citizen.

How might we understand religious equality?

There are two very different traditions in schools. Torevell et al. (2013) distinguish faith schools where values are intended to flow from God, and community schools that give primacy to ethical and humanist values, where God is an optional extra. Much of the discussion about religious equality in schools takes the second approach and stresses the necessity for children to be equipped with a self-aware, critical understanding of a range of religions in their society, tolerance and confidence in their freedom to practise a religion, should they choose to do so. The flavour of this stance is evident in the guidance for inspectors in England who judge a school by the degree to which pupils have an 'interest in exploring, improving understanding of and showing respect for different faiths' (Ofsted, 2015: 37).

However, whilst it is difficult to argue with the intent of such statements, they provide little guidance on what religious equality means when there are disagreements about, for example, how far differing religious practice should be accommodated in schools. In Europe, schools have varied policies on children wearing religious symbols and clothing. In France, for example, wearing religious symbols is not allowed, including the *niqab* (head covering which covers the face except the eyes) and the crucifix. The provision of alternatives to meals containing pork in schools is hotly contested (Bryant, 2015; Tissot, 2011). In Britain, whilst religious clothing is generally allowed, school policy is not always consistent. For example, in some schools students have been asked not to wear a cross or a head covering. These examples highlight policy and practice wavering between acceptance of difference and the desire to see others integrate into the practice of the majority. A third way sidesteps disagreements, to some degree, by taking a secular stance and finding common ground through promoting shared values.

Different approaches to achieving greater religious equality

The majority of schools endeavour to nurture a set of values that underpins the human right to religious freedom and spiritual development. Consequently, we consider how values are used in practice and approaches to religious and intercultural education. We also explore how equipping students to understand the psychology of fear and discrimination might contribute to creating positive attitudes to different faiths.

Values

Several of the case example schools stress the centrality of values in increasing equality. An example is Maclear School, which has new learners from many parts of the world arriving every week and addresses the issue of common values from the moment of enrolment. Staff refer both to general values such as courtesy and to their interpretation of British values such as the rule of law, and specifically to tolerance of different faiths. This is an example of making common values the central platform within which religious tolerance is embedded:

Maclear: values

We very much sell it, with the transition [into the school], very much talk about our values as being values that we can all work to in our school and actually they will serve you well in the rest of your life and are congruent with all the different religions and cultures ... Now that we've got the British values twist on it as well, again it sits with us ... It's our values, but it's human values more generally ... So this is our community, and these are the guides to the way we behave and treat each other and work together. People buy into that.

Enacting values is a constant challenge. In the view of Maclear's head teacher and curriculum director, it is not just deciding on values but also embedding them persistently with staff and with parents and students over years that builds a culture of equality:

Maclear: staff values

As you get new staff coming into the school you embed those values into them ... They come on board with the culture and the vision of the school, whereas previously there was a core group of staff that had been here for many years and had their own way.

Arriving at the current culture had taken Maclear School several years. The same emphasis was evident in St Mary's School. Whilst the values base is Catholic, the head teacher argued that the kind of values endorsed are argued to be relevant in any school:

St Mary's: values

When I interview the staff I'm interested in their core values. I can train people to teach. I can train them to mark books. What I can't do is change their core values. So what we work on is these values. We do it with our students. We do it with our parents and obviously we do it with our staff. Because creating a community and creating a functioning school is about us all working towards those particular values of which clearly achievement is at the top … but also the spirituality, you know, the type of person you are inside and how you deal with other people, respect and relationships, are all those keys to a quality of life … obviously the Catholic religion at this school is at the centre of that but you could equally operate those values in every school.

About 20 per cent of the pupils in this Catholic school are Muslim. The head teacher believed that many parents and children choose the school because they want a faith-based education. The formal faith may be Catholic, but the commonalities of faith in Catholicism and other religions are a central facet of the school values:

St Mary's: a faith-based education for those of different faiths

At the centre of all religion is a god … This school has never been 100 per cent Catholic and in my view it never should be, because it offers a faith-based education to families which is Catholic but it isn't exclusively Catholic. It's respecting of other families who come here because of faith.

A similar belief is evident in the case of the appointment of a Jewish head teacher to a Church of England school with a majority of Muslim pupils. What matters most in this instance, according to the Church of England's chief education officer, is not adherence to a particular religion but 'an understanding of the value and importance of faith' (Sherwood, 2015). This, in itself, is a value that can be shared across religions.

Holding the value of religious tolerance is a good springboard, yet it does not resolve the issue of how to act if children's or parents' beliefs or practice resulting from their interpretation of a religion conflict with the school's other values or with equality legislation. For example, at Maclear beliefs about gender are tackled head on, from the earliest moment:

Maclear: values in action

Occasionally when Year 7s arrive, some of the boys have got a particular view of women ... and I don't shy away. It's a difficult one but I've never had a parent come back to me. We'll tackle some boys and say, 'I hope you're not speaking to me like that because I'm a female' and I go into, you know, equality in this country and equal opportunity.

What this example highlights is that values do not in themselves resolve dilemmas about how to behave. In this case, one value – tolerance of practice in different faiths – conflicts with another value concerning gender equality. In handling this tension, the head teacher adopted a hierarchy of values, with equality legislation being the deciding factor. If, for example, particular interpretations of some religions, such as Islam, Orthodox Judaism and certain Christian sects, promote unequal roles for men and women, tolerance of such beliefs cannot override the commitment to gender equality embedded in British and European law.

Homosexuality is another area where values concerning tolerance appear to conflict with the law on equal rights. Practice in the Islamic and Catholic case example schools offers insight into how this plays out:

Rawabit: attitude to homosexuality

We teach that homosexuality exists and that some people choose it, but that Islam forbids it. As human beings we are not allowed to discriminate against people, but we would say to the children that if you know anyone like that you should advise them against it, but not deal differently with them ... You can't teach children that you hate people who do things you don't believe in.

Here, religious belief is made clear alongside an insistence that it should not lead to discrimination. A similar approach is evident in St Mary's School, where Catholic teaching is made clear but children are ultimately encouraged to be tolerant and accepting:

St Mary's: attitude to homosexuality

We have to set out very clearly that this is what the Catholic faith believes, and we try to explain why and we try to encourage children to follow that line of thinking, but at the end of the day as an individual you have the right to form a view … I work amongst Catholics and there may well be a creed but there's a wide church around that creed, so I will have Catholic staff here who do believe in abortion although the Catholic Church preaches something somewhat different. I do have people who believe in contraception who are practising Catholics. I do have people who are practising Catholics who are very comfortable with homosexuality, same-sex marriages, whereas the Church has a very different view on it … I am absolutely sure there are gay children in the school.

I'd hope it's openly discussed. I'd hope children feel encouraged to come forward and discuss it openly with our chaplain.

The head teacher emphasized that the priority is to equip pupils to leave the school and enter adult society with confidence. In the messy real world, both the law and children's human right to a nurturing environment prohibit the inflexible imposition of any religious teaching that may undermine children's confidence and self-respect.

If a values statement does not resolve dilemmas, nevertheless it is a start. Values offer a framework for discussion, negotiation and, when necessary, a final decision by leaders. When beliefs are deeply felt and differ profoundly it may not always be possible to reconcile these. In such circumstances, having a clear hierarchy of values is one means to navigate difficult territory.

Religious education

The emphasis on common or British values is not without its critics. The insistence from 2014 that schools consider what is meant by British values has met both support and resistance amongst school leaders and teachers. Some argue that the result is to privilege the perspective of the majority and to embed further the inequalities experienced by those of minority religions (Bhopal, 2012). To counter such a negative outcome, a critical understanding of the historical development of religions and how some have become privileged may help pupils understand the context and implications of a school's values. Religious education (RE) has a vital part to play.

Currently, there is widespread criticism that RE replicates inequalities rather than reduces them. Just as in Chapter 8 it is emphasized that schools need to go beyond challenging homophobia and to replace heterosexuality as the norm, in aspiring to religious equality it is not enough to counter discrimination against those of a particular religion. A privileged European and Christian perspective can be challenged. As Andraos (2012) points out, the common strategies of the addition of different readings and different voices, including occasional visitors from a range of cultural perspectives, may not be enough to make the curriculum less Christian and Euro-centric.

The head teacher of Rawabit School reflected on his experience that allowing children to absent themselves from an activity on religious grounds merely means they miss an educational activity, and argued for a curriculum that is accessible to all:

Rawabit: RE curriculum

I have inspected over 100 schools and there is a lot of inequality in respect of the curriculum, what is actually being taught ... For example when Christmas time is coming up there are lots of activities based around the nativity. It can even be included in literacy, history and geography, areas that are important to every child. They (Muslim children) become disengaged because what they are learning is at odds with their beliefs.

A religious practice that is beneficial to primary school kids is making Christmas cards – that would be a religious practice. Why instead can't a child make a card for their mum, perhaps a 'thank you' card? They would be practising all the same skills.

This debate inspires heated proponents on all sides. Some argue that if a state is predominantly Christian, this should be embedded in the curriculum. Others, as the head teacher above, argue that no aspect of the curriculum in a community school should exclude any children. The central question is one of inclusion and how children experience their school if they are disengaged by particular activities or must absent themselves. There is no single answer, particularly when a school has children of many different religions and sects. Just as legislation is an overriding imperative, so inclusion is a touchstone that may help to resolve such debate.

Staff may require considerable development in order to achieve religious inclusion. Teachers are not always equipped with an appropriate depth of knowledge and understanding. Given the relatively higher level of negativity towards Muslims (Francis et al., 2015), this is particularly critical in relation to Islam. Teachers and head teachers also often lack basic awareness about Islam (Shah, 2006). Where teaching about this religion is included in the curriculum, Panjwani identifies a range of shortcomings:

> the *sharia* is rarely discussed through a historical lens; neglect of intra-Muslim diversity, particularly the doctrinal diversity among Muslims; and the oversimplified presentation of the role and appropriation of foundational Islamic texts such as the Qur'an. (Panjwani, 2014: 9)

In both community and faith schools, children and young people can be equipped with a critical and political understanding of how world faiths have developed and how far they have enjoyed equality or the contrary. Such an education seems rare, currently. Dinham and Shaw (2015) surveyed learners, parents and teachers. The groups agreed on the importance of RE, but shared disappointment at its status within the curriculum and, in particular, the often inadequate time it is allocated. Learners nearly all felt inadequately equipped to respond to stereotypes and misinformation in the media. Nearly all wished to study a wide range of religions and felt that their current focus on just one or two did not allow them to engage with a diverse society in the positive way that they wished. The findings of this survey suggest that many schools are not fulfilling their role in supporting religious equality.

Intercultural education

In this section we discuss intercultural education. The terms 'multicultural' and 'intercultural' education are sometimes used synonymously and sometimes to indicate different values or approaches (Grant and Portera, 2011). In broad brush, we interpret multicultural approaches as encompassing increased knowledge of diverse groups with the aim of reducing inequality. Intercultural education is defined in many different ways, but here we assume that it places emphasis on equipping individuals with the skills to function positively as members of a diverse society. At its core is an understanding that '"an information package on other cultures" is totally inadequate for learning how to live, and live in a *good* way, in an ethnically and culturally diverse society' (Leeman, 2003: 32). The aim is to go beyond merely informing learners about the culture, beliefs and practice of others, and to give them the skills and understanding to be more self-aware of their response to differences amongst people. In effect, intercultural education emphasizes both engaging with difference and understanding the psychology of how we respond to difference.

There are examples throughout Europe of initiatives that aim to encourage children and young people to step into the shoes of others, and develop their understanding of relations between groups. Such strategies relate not just to different religions but also to other kinds of discrimination, such as racism. Given the connections made by many between religion and ethnicity, children need to understand how negative attitudes to particular religious and ethnic groups are formed, and where they can lead. Intercultural education therefore aims to replace ignorance, prejudice, fear and hate with empathy, critical thinking, self-esteem and respect.

Examples of intercultural education include an initiative in a town in the Netherlands experiencing high levels of violence by young people against refugees. An exchange between Dutch and Polish secondary students, including a visit to Auschwitz, aimed to increase the understanding of where attacks against those of a particular religion or race can lead. In France, where both anti-semitism and Islamophobia appear to be growing, the Coexist organization provides safe spaces for young people to explore their stereotypes of other groups and how the latter may see them. In both of these initiatives, the psychology of in-groups and out-groups is explicitly explored, allowing children to understand the powerful impulse to think positively of one's own group and negatively of those who seem 'other'. They are encouraged to look back critically through history, including recent history, to consider the sometimes horrific results of the fundamental human impetus to protect the in-group and to attack out-groups.

An education in the psychology of scapegoating, fear and attitudes to minorities is not a minor extra to be included, if possible, in personal and social education or even RE, but should be embedded as a foundational aspect of providing religious equality within schools and beyond. Many school leaders are frustrated that, despite high-level European and national policy that rhetorically emphasizes education for citizenship and religious tolerance, the focus of policy makers seems primarily on achievement standards, crowding out a broader education (Trethewey and Menzies, n.d.).

Despite such frustration, a hope was expressed at the 2015 European Commission Education, Training and Youth Forum that a better world is only ever one generation away. If our children can be educated to be confident, self-aware and tolerant, a more peaceful world is within our grasp in the foreseeable future.

Picking a way forward

Many reading this chapter will do so from the perspective of the religion to which they are committed, or from a humanist or secular stance. No doubt they will detect a bias depending on their perspective. Writing about religious equality for such a diverse audience in both community and faith schools is highly challenging. Yet it is just this kind of challenge that school leaders and teachers face: they must accommodate those who practise a range of religions; those who wish schools to privilege one religion; and those who believe schools should be secular. How, then, might increasing inequality in relation to religion be understood?

Religious equality, as discussed in this chapter, is not only about the human right to practise one's religion, but also about religious education in its broad sense as a tool to develop confident, tolerant citizens in a diverse society. The situation often demands, rather than invites, compromise and flexibility, as is shown in the following case example. To enrol at St Mary's, pupils and their parents must sign that their children will 'share in the full Catholic life of the school':

St Mary's: worship

We have a number of Muslims here who will not say the 'Hail Mary' and will not say the 'Our Father'. They obviously don't take Communion. However, they still come to Mass.

We would never have an Islamic service here, because that's not what the foundation of the school is, but my staff are not challenging students who are not joining in the 'Hail Mary' but are sitting respectfully and quietly and prayerfully, possibly praying to their own God whoever that is, and that is all absolutely acceptable. We do have one or two children who actually sit with the Koran whilst we're sat in Mass and that's perfectly acceptable in the ethos that we are developing within the school, because we're developing religious tolerance.

Whatever your reaction to this practice, it is easy to discern the complex web of circumstance that confronts this head teacher. Parents wish their children to have a faith-based education, but there are no alternative local faith schools. The head teacher and the staff wish to respect and enact the foundation values of the school, which are Catholic, but also need to respect those students who practise another faith. There are no easy answers to what religious equality looks like in such circumstances, only difficult choices.

School leaders struggle with how best to enable children and young people to fulfil the expectation of the majority that religion is a force for good in the world, and to grow up confident that they may practise their religion, or no religion, in the expectation of giving and receiving respect, whatever their gender, ethnicity or sexuality. Inevitably, neat, tidy solutions are not available. Two possible sources of guidance have been suggested:

- Holding a clear hierarchy of values of which those embedded in equality legislation are the most important, as this offers protection against discrimination and unequal chances to all citizens in a democratic society.
- Striving for inclusion; that is, considering the perspective of religious minorities within the school community and trying to ensure that the curriculum and all aspects of the school experience are as welcoming and pertinent to them as to the majority.

Leaders in schools with children of many different faiths might smile wryly at this depiction of what may seem 'mission: impossible'. However, our exploration of practice in schools leads us to believe in the creativity and commitment of staff who, if they cannot find a perfect solution that satisfies all, find the optimum way in the most testing environments.

Key actions

- Establish a set of values that can be used as a touchstone for common expectations of behaviour throughout the school. Be clear on the hierarchy amongst these values.
- Work consistently to embed such values in practice.
- In community schools, consider the degree to which one religion or worldview, most often Christianity, is privileged and develop the curriculum to be more balanced. In faith schools, ensure children have a critical understanding of how their own faith has developed and its relationship to other faiths.

- Develop all staff to ensure a more in-depth understanding of the nature and range of religions within the school to avoid offence or superficial and inappropriate homogenizing of diverse groups under single labels, such as Christian, Muslim or Jewish.
- Explicitly educate children to understand the psychology of religious intolerance and to develop critical self-awareness and empathy.

For reflection and discussion

Select a minority religion within your school. Consider what the experience of a child with that religion might be and how far the school offers that child religious equality. Depending on how far you are satisfied, think about how religious equality might be better secured for children of minority religions.

Additional reading

For consideration of religious education:

DfES (2005) *Higher Standards, Better Schools for All* (White Paper). London: HMSO.

Dinham, A. and Shaw, M. (2015) *REforREal: The Future of Teaching and Learning About Religion and Belief*. London: Culham St Gabriel's/Goldsmiths.

Francis, L.J., Pyke, A. and Penny, G. (2015) 'Christian affiliation, Christian practice, and attitudes to religious diversity: a quantitative analysis among 13- to 15-year-old female students in the UK', *Journal of Contemporary Religion*, 30 (2): 249–63.

Panjwani, F. (2014) 'Beyond the saga of the "Trojan horse": some reflections on teaching about Islam in schools', *The Middle East in London*, 10 (5): 9.

RE online (2012) *Religious Education in Europe*. www.reonline.org.uk/news/religious-education-in-europe/ (accessed 04.05.16).

Research on Religion and Education in Europe, REDCo Project (Religion, Education, Dialogue, Conflict). http://aulre.org/

For consideration of intercultural education:

National Union of Teachers (n.d.) *Anti-Semitism in the UK: A Submission to the All-Party Parliamentary Inquiry into Anti-Semitism in the UK from the National Union of Teachers*. www.teachers.org.uk/files/Anti-Semitism_4424.pdf (accessed 02.11.15).

Trethewey, A. and Menzies, L. (n.d.) *Encountering Faiths and Beliefs: The Role of Intercultural Education in Schools and Communities*. www.3ff.org.uk/documents/reports/encounteringfaithsbeliefs2015.pdf (accessed 04.05.16).

UNESCO (n.d.) *Fighting Islamophobia in Schools*. www.unesco.org/new/en/education/resources/in-focus-articles/fighting-islamophobia-in-schools/ (accessed 04.05.16).

Zine, J. (2001) 'Muslim youth in Canadian schools: education and the politics of religious identity', *Anthropology & Education Quarterly*, 32 (4): 399–423.

For consideration on the place of faith schools:

Accord Coalition (2016) *Databank of Independent Evidence on Faith Schools* (March) http://accordcoalition.org.uk/wp-content/uploads/2013/12/Databank-of-Independent-Evidence-on-Faith-Schools-April-2014.pdf (accessed 04.05.16).

Allen, R. and West, A. (2011) 'Why do faith secondary schools have advantaged intakes? The relative importance of neighbourhood characteristics, social background and religious identification amongst parents', *British Educational Research Journal*, 37 (4): 691–712.

Patrikios, S. and Curtice, J. (2014) 'Attitudes towards school choice and faith schools in the UK: a question of individual preference or collective interest?', *Journal of Social Policy*, 43 (3): 517–34.

For consideration of Islamophobia:

Shah, S. and Shaikh, J. (2010) 'Leadership progression of Muslim male teachers: interplay of ethnicity, faith and visibility', *School Leadership and Management*, 30 (1): 19–33.

Shain, F. (2011) *The New Folk Devils: Muslim Boys and Education in England*. Stoke-on-Trent: Trentham Books.

Sian, K.P. (2015) 'Spies, surveillance and stakeouts: monitoring Muslim moves in British state schools', *Race Ethnicity and Education*, 18 (2): 183–201.

Vryonides, M. (2014) 'Interethnic violence in schools across European countries', in M. Sedmak, Z. Medaric and S. Walker (eds), *Children's Voices: Studies of Interethnic Conflict and Violence in European Schools*. Abingdon: Routledge, pp. 49–63.

11

Migrant children and equality

Migrants – that is, anyone who was born outside the country in which they reside – have been an issue of worldwide interest for some time. In 2013 the United Nations calculated that there were 232 million migrants globally, and that 'at the heart of this phenomenon are human beings in search of decent work and a better or safer life' (United Nations General Assembly, 2013: 4). A surge in migrants trying to enter Europe has pushed migration to the top of the European political agenda. The sheer scale has challenged national policy and capacity. As a consequence, public attitudes to migrants vary, but the majority agree that the well-being of children is paramount and that migrant children must receive an appropriate education.

This chapter focuses on equality and the experience of migrant children in school. An intersectionality approach, as discussed in Chapter 3, recognizes that the experience of each child is not shaped by a single characteristic, as here their migrant status, but by several characteristics intersecting in a particular context. Given that many migrants are likely to encounter issues not just because they are migrants, but also in response to their ethnicity or religion, some of the issues they face may overlap with those discussed in other chapters of the book. In this chapter we consider the perspective of migrants, but you will also find relevant ideas in the chapters on socioeconomic status, ethnicity and religion.

In this chapter we ask you to think about:

- the community context and migrants' relationships with peers and staff
- the achievement of migrant children compared to others

(Continued)

(Continued)

- the factors that research suggests impact on migrant children's educational achievement
- developing learning for migrant children, including discussion of:
  - ability grouping
  - the curriculum
  - working with parents.

Case examples to illustrate points are drawn from three co-educational schools: Parrys Community Primary (3–11) in Wales; Maclear Community School (11–16), in a city in the south of England; and Tulback Academy (11–18), in inner London.

Migration: a hot topic

Providing a definitive picture of the number and nature of migrants is difficult. As the Migration Observatory at Oxford points out, there is no consensus on who counts as a migrant, and whether we should include children who are born in the UK but whose parents are foreign-born or foreign nationals (Anderson and Blinder, 2015). For the purpose of this chapter, we see an exact definition as less important than recognition that a growing number of children are from families that see themselves as migrants. Approximately 1.3 million migrants enter Europe each year. In the UK, the 2011 census found that 17.3 million (13 per cent) of usual residents were born outside the UK. About a third of London's inhabitants are migrants. In most of the rest of England the percentage is around 4 to 6 per cent. Scotland, Wales, the North-East and Northern Ireland have a lower percentage of migrants but, as in England, have clusters of higher concentration. Those arriving include people who took desperate risks to reach Europe; 464,000 migrants arrived by sea in the first nine months of 2015 (Council on Foreign Relations, 2015). The BBC reported over 3,000 deaths during migration in 2014 and 1,700 in just the months January to April 2015 ('Mediterranean migrants', 2015). All over Europe, schools receive children who may have been traumatized or orphaned by war or their parents' attempt to achieve a safer or better life for them.

Using the term 'migrant' as if it indicated a homogeneous group is misleading. Statistics for each country in the European Union show great variation in the country of birth, economic status and language of migrants

(European Migration Network, 2011). Similarly, schools' engagement with migrants varies. Some have few or no migrants and others many. The nature of the intake of migrants can impact considerably on schools' experience of meeting these children's needs, depending on factors such as language status, whether the arrival of migrants is staggered or not and the diversity of ethnicity.

Perceptions of migration and migrants are shaped by media coverage to a greater extent than many policy areas. Consequently, the environment in which migrant children go to school may reflect the negative perceptions evident in much press coverage. Embedded in the narratives about migrants are beliefs that they overwhelm aspects of public services, such as housing, health services and schools. Such fears were found to be unjustified by a UK Home Office report:

> Research and statistical evidence have shown that the presence of migrant children in schools has no negative effect on the attainment of non-migrant pupils ... and can, if anything, have a positive effect on general school and pupil performance. (Poppleton et al., 2013: 34)

Rather than the common narrative in the press of schools being disadvantaged by sudden large arrivals of migrants, it would seem that such children potentially have a positive effect on the school generally and its attainment levels.

The achievement of migrant children

The experience of each child and each school is unique, but there are issues that appear frequently. Migrant children are likely to suffer disadvantages that may seriously impact on their educational outcomes and future life chances (Darmody et al., 2014):

> With some exceptions, immigrant students, on average, have weaker education outcomes at all levels of education. They often have more restricted access to quality education; are less likely to participate in pre-primary education; more prone to drop out before completing upper secondary; more apt to have lower academic scores. (OECD, 2009: n.p.n.)

There is a performance gap between non-migrant and first-generation migrant children; the latter lag behind by an average of 1.5 years (OECD, 2007). The gap is assumed by many to be due to a lack of facility in the language of their host country, or their socioeconomic background, or both. In some countries, however, when research has taken socioeconomic background into account, no performance gap exists. Similarly, when research takes into account the home language, migrants show varying levels of performance in different countries. In those with a history of welcoming migrants, such as Canada, New Zealand and Australia, outcomes do not reflect poorer results for migrants. In other words, socioeconomic background and language may partly explain the attainment gap, but it is clear that national cultures, policies and the actions of schools are also part of its cause (Moskal, 2014).

The gap is even more disturbing when you take into account that many principals and teachers report that, on arrival, migrant children often have higher levels of motivation, aspiration and achievement than others in the school (Darmody et al., 2014). The head teacher and curriculum director of Maclear School, which receives new children every week from many countries throughout the world, noted how some migrants were jubilant at their first experience of school:

Maclear: learners' joy at being in school

I'm thinking of the group of girls who are probably now in Year 11 who came from Bangladesh in Year 9, had no English and hadn't been to school before, and they were very much linked to the EAL team. But to those girls it was just amazing, I think they were just joyous in school because, gosh can you image being brought here and being able to be a child?

She also notes the sheer pleasure of small boys being able to enjoy the space in the school, where before they may have been confined to living in rooms with nowhere to run around. Such children are often hungry to use the opportunity of education and, as the head teacher of Maclear insists, are well able to do so. The examination outcomes of the school provide a clear illustration that migrant children, and in particular those with English as an additional language, can achieve as well or better than those born in the host country and, rather than disadvantaging their school, can be a positive asset.

Segregation and teacher diversity

Chapter 2 considered the way that national policy impacts on issues of equality. School choice exacerbates segregation and this, in turn, shapes the experience of migrants as choice options for them are likely to be narrowly limited. High-attaining schools are generally oversubscribed. Those schools that recruit from a local catchment where migrants are not housed or that prioritize a specific faith may, in effect, exclude migrants. In some cases, schools are able to select the highest attainers, further discriminating against migrants who struggle to demonstrate attainment when they first reach a new country. Nusche (2009: 10) points to an example in Sweden where allowing independent schools to choose entrants by ability led to 'a marked increase in segregation across schools by immigration status'.

School choice also allows parents to opt out of schools that have a high proportion of migrant students (Bloem and Diaz, 2007). The percentage of migrants to trigger such flight from a school varies from 35–40 per cent in Denmark to 50–60 per cent in the Netherlands. The net result is a spiral where migrant segregation is exacerbated. Throughout Europe, migrants are concentrated in schools with a high level of disadvantaged learners, and the UK is notable for being at the bottom of this particular OECD league table, with 80 per cent of migrants in schools that have many students from disadvantaged backgrounds (OECD, 2012).

Reynolds (2008) suggests that it is vital for students to be able to 'identity match' to other learners and to staff, and this is clearly relevant to migrants as well as other minority groups of learners. The problem is that the increasing diversity amongst learners in schools due to the arrival of migrant children is not reflected in staffing. It may be difficult or impossible to adjust staffing fast enough to respond to dramatic shifts in the school demographic profile – that is, change that is both sudden and large scale – and there is a long-term underlying problem. Teachers from diverse ethnic and religious backgrounds remain under-represented (see Chapters 4 and 9). This situation impacts directly on migrants in that there may be too few teachers and leaders with experience of different cultures or language and, indirectly, in that role models other than White men and women may be absent.

In summary, the context in which migrant children enter schools is one where securing equality is deeply problematic. They are likely to be segregated with children from disadvantaged backgrounds, and have few or no members of staff with whom they can identify.

Staff response

It is assumed that staff welcome migrant children into schools; this is not always the case. Teachers generally believe that they are supportive of all children and do not exhibit any kind of prejudice, but this may be optimistic.

Evidence suggests that teachers may unthinkingly hold negative views about particular groups of learners (Reynolds, 2008). Devine (2013) found that staff in Irish schools tended to assess migrants on the basis of their behaviour rather than their cognitive ability. If they were no trouble and had middle-class attitudes towards education and work, they were welcomed positively; where migrant status intersected with poor socioeconomic background or minority ethnicity, the welcome was often less warm: 'Teachers tended to be most positive about those children who were most like themselves' (Devine, 2013: 288). Even if prejudices or stereotypical views are absent, limited ability in English may also lead to underestimation of a migrant's ability. Staff attitudes based on inaccurate estimates of ability and ethnic stereotypes not only may make migrant children feel isolated and vulnerable but can have serious implications for their learning opportunities. Nusche (2009) notes that in Swiss schools over 50 per cent of children in special classes and special schools are not of Swiss nationality, and that in some other European countries migrant children are moved into special education much more quickly than those born in the host country.

In some schools, having English as an additional language creates expectations of poor performance and, when children fail to progress, is accepted as the cause, a self-fulfilling prophecy. This is not the case everywhere. As the head teacher and curriculum director of Maclear School pointed out, having English as an additional language is no reason for children not attaining at high levels:

Maclear: expectations of migrants

When you look at individual case studies of students who are making huge amounts of progress, when they join us to when they leave, that's all the evidence you need. That's the progress.

We have really high expectations of all the students. So in terms of the targets for their subjects, EAL students, along with everybody else, are expected to make very high levels of progress and in a sense we will not allow any member of staff to say 'that child hasn't done it in my subject because this is their second language'.

The school's latest inspection report confirms the outstanding progress made by many migrant learners in the school, leading to higher GCSE results than the national average.

Schools therefore face a number of challenges in relation to staffing to meet the needs of migrant children:

1. Increasing the diversity of staff.
2. Training all staff in order to raise awareness and increase ability to respond to children of varying ethnicity, religion and culture.
3. Training staff in teaching techniques to support language development in all curriculum areas.

The first challenge is particularly problematic. Many highly experienced teachers tend to self-select into schools in more affluent areas where there are fewer migrants. Recruitment of minority ethnic staff is easiest in metropolitan or other areas where the surrounding population is diverse. There are no easy answers.

The US is further on than Europe in training staff to support diverse learners and their language development. The national percentage of English language learners in the US is around 10 per cent: that is, 5.4 million (Batalova and McHugh, 2010). The rapidly rising number has impelled engagement with how to support such children. The most usual means, running professional workshops, has been widely recognized as ineffective. Newman et al. (2010: 154) suggest that to up-skill teachers effectively, in-service training needs to be 'sustained and continuous, rather than brief and decontextualized, and promote learning communities and collaboration'. Effective development of staff is likely to look quite different from workshops. Though devised some time ago, Kutner's (1992) principles that describe the necessary elements still hold good: that theory and research need to be incorporated; that practice must be demonstrated and practised in safe spaces; that support is needed for new methods to be tried more than once; and that such development must be ongoing and not 'one off' (adapted from Kutner, 1992: n.p.n.).

In these times of frenzied pressure, it is difficult to build a community of practice within a school or cluster of schools in the way described. However, given that the alternative is having staff firefight problems that emerge because the school is not meeting the needs of migrant children, such sustained development may save time in the longer term.

Relationships in school

Relationships between children can be tense. This may particularly be the case when the school has two, rather than many, ethnic groups. A binary appears to highlight division, whilst many boundaries between groups may blur distinctions, as in Tulback School:

Tulback: integration of groups

We have a range of ethnic groups in the school which means that we don't have a specific challenge unlike for instance a school with a large African-Caribbean population where you might get a challenge around that group. If you have lots of different ethnicities the school becomes more mixed and you don't get groups who hang together. It is more of an indistinguishable community.

However, while migrants from many countries attending a school may reduce discrimination and conflict, some groups may experience a particularly negative response. For example, in one case study school Reynolds (2008) found that relationships between migrant Roma children and other learners were very poor. Parents, too, can contribute to divisions. Staff at Parrys School in Wales encountered a situation faced by many schools:

Parrys: parental relations

Arrival of central European children without any prior notice resulted in the school trying to integrate pupils with no preschool experience into school life. The added pressure was the Czech Republic families not speaking to the Roma Czech families. The school needed to put emergency plans into place to assist new families to understand school, the school system and school life.

Positive relationships with both peers and staff are crucial for children's learning. In Parrys School a number of actions have been taken to try to ease tension and draw migrant children and their families into a sense of belonging. The school ensured an immediate sense of welcome by offering application forms written in the home language, followed by support in the home language. They also provided a nurture room as a safe space to assist new arrivals to settle into the school system (Bennathan and Boxall, 2010):

Parrys: helping children and their families settle in

The result was the Family Nurture Room – a safe secure place for new arrivals to have necessary support to help them settle into school life. The Nurture Room is accessed by those who require support settling into school. They spend every morning in the Nurture Room following the classic nurture group routine and principles. Two afternoons a week their families attend class to learn alongside their child. One afternoon is a focus on basic science language – weather, parts of the body, etc., and the second afternoon is a celebration of the learning that has taken place during the week. This has provided a forum for staff to arrange visits from dentists, doctors, opticians, etc. to speak to new arrival families.

This example is a primary school where language acquisition and adaptation may be swifter than with older learners. In secondary schools, for psychological and physical safety migrant children can limit relationships to their own ethnic groups. They also sometimes seek out friends for whom English is the home language to facilitate their language learning. In Reynolds' (2008) case study, a policy of deliberate seating plans ensured that migrants had proximity to those from their home country, but not exclusively, to counter the tendency to cluster together. Other initiatives were evident, such as encouraging migrants to join after-school clubs and sports, all based on an acute awareness of shaping relationships to the advantage of migrant children and also benefiting all. Providing an organizational culture and social context in which migrant children can thrive is the foundation for leaders to build curriculum, pedagogy and assessment strategies to include everyone.

Developing learning for migrants

A number of challenges face leaders, including how to place migrant children in classes or groups, developing the curriculum and working with parents.

Ability grouping

Ability grouping is used extensively throughout Europe with the goal of creating a class teaching environment with less diverse needs (Nusche, 2009: 12). No doubt many reading this chapter will have heard this argument rehearsed frequently. Commonly, staff and parents fear that inclusion of children perceived as of lesser attainment in mixed ability groups, and particularly those whose English language is poor, will depress the overall standard of achievement of the group and the children perceived as of lesser attainment will struggle to keep up, as discussed in Chapter 6.

However, assessment prior to a decision on placement in sets or streams is problematic. There is ample evidence that teachers' judgements are often biased (Schölmerich et al., 2008) and, even if they were not, assessing a child's ability is difficult when he or she may be suffering the effects of, at best, dislocation and, at worst, family loss and trauma. Add the impact of inadequately developed language of instruction, in many cases, and the reasons are evident for the disproportionate allocation of migrant children to special classes and groups projected to attain less.

Ability grouping is so embedded in many schools that it is a taken-for-granted practice, assumed to be based on objective assessment and leading to optimum instruction for all. Evidence suggests that this is not the case (Field et al., 2007). Gamoran (2010: 217) concluded that, 'with few exceptions, the evidence indicates that tracking (*ability grouping*) tends to magnify inequality'. There are many reasons why this is the case. Gamoran identifies some that are vital:

> A number of studies have concluded that students in higher tracks encounter more challenging curricula, move at a faster pace, and are taught by more experienced teachers with better reputations, whilst students in low tracks encounter more fragmented, worksheet-oriented, and slower-paced instruction provided by teachers with less experience or clout. (2010: 217)

Two responses are important. One is to train teachers so that their assessment is less biased. This offers an advantage in providing more accurate information on the migrant's learning needs on arrival in school. The second is to take account of the evidence that gains, if any, for the advantaged are more than offset by losses for the disadvantaged, and to remove such selective grouping. Removing or limiting ability grouping is one of the key steps recommended by the OECD to achieve greater equity, as they define it, in schools. It is of especial importance to migrants, given that their placement is likely to be significantly influenced not by their ability but by their standard in the language of instruction.

Removing grouping by ability will be difficult for many leaders. Gamoran (2010), drawing on Oakes (1992), identified three challenges: overcoming people's beliefs that ability grouping works best; overcoming vested interests such as resistance from parents of high-attaining children or teachers who like teaching able groups; and overcoming the technical difficulties of achieving a pedagogy that sufficiently differentiates.

Most argue on the basis of the first – that is, educational arguments – thereby disguising even from themselves a stance that may be based on the second: vested interests. Teachers may not welcome the challenge of teaching diverse groups. Heterogeneous classes are much harder work and may feel less satisfying. However, without tackling this structural aspect of inequality, schools will be hindered in increasing equality for migrants.

Developing the curriculum

The curriculum often reflects the cultural assumptions, history and social structures of the host nation. Schools make efforts to adjust the curriculum in response to their learners' experience, including migrants, to a greater or lesser degree. Migrants' geographical, religious and language knowledge are all strengths that can be used. Celebration events where learners have an opportunity to showcase their culture can be highly positive, but are no substitute for a curriculum that includes the perspective and experience of all. In Reynolds' (2008) case study, staff ensured that a considerable amount of Black history was taught so that migrants saw history as relevant: 'Migrant students learn and adapt to school culture more readily when their home culture is recognized and serves as a basis for instruction' (Romanowski, 2003: 31).

However, Romanowski suggests that initiatives based on a superficial understanding of culture may merely leave learners confused. For example, an anti-bullying programme intended to reduce bullying of migrants, suggesting that physical self-defence was inappropriate, appeared to the bullied further to disrespect their culture, in which standing up for yourself is fundamental. Accordingly, teachers learned that they needed to understand migrant cultures better and to design a curriculum that 'builds on migrant students' strengths and connects to their unique life experiences or prior knowledge' (Romanowski, 2003: 31).

Developing language

It is key to ensure that language development is built into all parts of the curriculum, rather than just being specialist EAL provision. In primary schools, McEachron and Bhatti (2005: 170) found: 'In terms of leadership ... the responsibility for looking after the day to-day linguistic needs of EAL students was mostly delegated by the principal to the Special Educational Needs Coordinator (SENCo). This implied that EAL learners' needs were seen not as an asset but as requiring special needs help':

Quite often it is the SENCo who feels the pressure to provide support for student needs most intensely. SENCos then have to balance this demand against the needs of other students with special needs such as dyslexia, dyspraxia and autism. It would be fair to say that there is a discrepancy between what is available to students in terms of their entitlement, and what can actually be managed on a day-to-day basis in school. (2005: 174)

Some additional help was available occasionally from the local mosque or trainee EAL teachers. Long-serving teaching assistants often became more skilled than teachers, but without their salary or promotion prospects. In the classroom some teachers welcomed interaction with EAL speakers. Others saw this as an interruption to the pursuit of learning goals. In the schools studied by McEachron and Bhatti (2005), teachers were expected to keep up with EAL developments, yet little training was provided.

Part of the answer is appropriate resources, but this is not the only issue. A positive attitude to migrant children's EAL needs is a precursor to building an integrated strategy for language support that marries specialist EAL teaching to language development, throughout the curriculum. Given the intellectual and cultural benefit to children of having two languages, and that one in six primary school pupils and over one in eight in secondary schools in England do not have English as their home language, meeting their needs is a central function of schools, not an add-on (NALDIC, 2015).

Working with parents

Much research suggests that school leaders recognize how crucial the relationship with family may be in supporting a child's learning, but are often frustrated by limited contact with parents (Lynch and Baker, 2005). As Nusche (2009: 33) points out, though often valuing education highly and communicating high aspirations to their children, migrant parents face particular problems in interacting with the school, 'such as language difficulties, weak knowledge in school subjects or lack of time and/or money to invest in their children's education. They may also feel alienated and unwelcome in a foreign school environment'. Moreover, they may face heartrending issues within the family:

We are worried, because our children neglect us, they are aggressive toward us, and they let us know often that we are stupid and unsuccessful compared with their Scottish peers' parents. They are ashamed of us because we do not speak English well ... They reject their roots, their parents, and their family, and that allows them to be accepted by their Scottish peers. (Moskal, 2014: 286)

The faster adaptation of children than their parents to a new language and culture can cause serious family conflict. The economic and social issues faced by many migrant families are also of a qualitatively greater magnitude than those of most families in the host country.

Working with migrant parents cannot, therefore, rely on the kind of guidelines and processes suggested in relation to generic parental involvement. There is relatively little research that can help, but one study of a number of schools in the US found common factors in those schools that had had a degree of success (López et al., 2001). All staff were consistently and persistently committed to meeting the needs of the family, seeing this as indivisible from meeting the needs of the child, as exemplified in Parrys School in Wales. In the schools in four districts in the US study, cross-agency working to muster the help and support needed by families was an essential first step before the parents could be expected to focus on engagement with the school. In each school, staff were trained and at least one adult came to know the life story of each migrant family. Only by knowing the context of the wider economic and social needs of the family was it possible to understand why a child was able to work and achieve, or not (López et al., 2001). An example of such close contact with the families of migrant learners is provided by a case study of a school in Manchester (Ofsted, 2014b: 24):

> On the first day, the children arrived with no food and no money. The school provided a meal and asked the parents for payment. This pattern continued for the second and third day, with no payment received by the school. On the third day, staff took the children home. The parent said there was no food in the house so staff waited at home with the children while the parent bought food. The children were taken back to school where they ate their meals.

> On the fourth day, the pattern was repeated and the children were taken home. On the fifth day, the children arrived with an empty lunchbox. Again a home visit was made.

> In the second week, the lunchbox contained some food but not enough for three children. This time the staff went with the parent to a budget supermarket and advised them on cheap, healthy food. The pattern continued for a few more days, but eventually the children started to bring enough food.

The majority of head teachers do not believe they have, as yet, established such close contact with migrant families (Wilkin et al., 2010). There are sources of ideas for practice offered at the end of this chapter. Most emphasize that action was developed despite funding cuts. It would seem that some schools, however challenging the financial and social context, find ways of reaching out to migrant families to the benefit of students.

Key actions

A number of areas of practice have been reviewed in this chapter. Of necessity these are selective, but nevertheless some key points have emerged as ideas to meet the needs of migrant learners better:

- Call for the persistent commitment of all staff long term, not just specialist teachers.
- Develop staff to understand different cultures and to implement EAL support.
- Work with migrant families in a different way from other groups of parents, understanding that engaging with the context of migrant children's lives is fundamental.
- Shape the social and academic contact of migrants with other learners in class and more widely to avoid isolation and counter racism.
- Adapt the curriculum to build on the strengths of migrant learners and embed relevance to their cultures and experiences.
- Embed EAL development as an integrated curriculum-wide requirement, and not just the province of the SENCo or specialist staff.

Schools may face difficult challenges in confronting society's often negative or hostile attitudes to migrants, which are imported into schools by learners, parents and, sometimes, staff. The case examples presented here provide evidence that migrants can be a rich addition that advantages everyone in a school. It is leadership's task to establish a positive culture where, to paraphrase the Swann Report (1985), it is not a question of educating migrant children, but of educating all children to their mutual benefit.

For reflection and discussion

What measures has your school or department taken to support positive social relations between migrant and other learners? What more might be done?

   Are the needs of migrant children integrated in the curriculum and teaching or a peripheral add-on? What development might further embed meeting their needs?

Additional reading

Darmody, M., Byrne D. and McGinnity, F. (2014) 'Cumulative disadvantage? Educational careers of migrant students in Irish secondary schools', *Race, Ethnicity and Education*, 17 (1): 129–51.

Devine, D. (2013) '"Value"ing children differently? Migrant children in education', *Children & Society*, 27 (4): 282–94.

López, G.R., Scribner, J.D. and Mahitivanichcha, K. (2001) 'Redefining parental involvement: lessons from high-performing migrant-impacted schools', *American Educational Research Journal*, 38 (2): 253–88.

McEachron, G. and Bhatti, G. (2005) 'Language support for immigrant children: a study of state schools in the UK and US', *Language, Culture and Curriculum*, 18 (2): 164–80.

Moskal, M. (2014) 'Polish migrant youth in Scottish schools: conflicted identity and family capital', *Journal of Youth Studies*, 17 (2): 279–91.

Reynolds, G. (2008) 'The impacts and experiences of migrant children in UK secondary schools', Working Paper No 47. Brighton: University of Sussex, Sussex Centre for Migration Research, pp. 1–34. www.sussex.ac.uk/webteam/gateway/file.php?name=mwp47.pdf&site=252 (accessed 05.05.16).

Additional resources

A case study of EAL support in a preschool playgroup:

www.surreycc.gov.uk/schools-and-learning/childcare-professionals/early-years-foundation-stage-eyfs/communication-and-language-in-the-eyfs/supporting-your-children-with-english-as-an-additional-language (accessed 09.05.16).

Examples of EAL support in Scotland:

www.educationscotland.gov.uk/inclusionandequalities/additionalsupportforlearning/eal/sharingpractice.asp (accessed 05.05.16).

www.educationscotland.gov.uk/inclusionandequalities/additionalsupportforlearning/eal/resources.asp (accessed 05.05.16).

Containing case studies from a number of schools in relation to Roma children:

Ofsted (2014) *Overcoming Barriers: Ensuring that Roma children are Fully Engaged and Achieving in Education*. London: HMI.

12

Special learning needs, disability and equality

Special learning needs and disability pose challenges for leaders of schools grappling with ideas of equality, equity and inclusion, and how to apply them. Equality implying sameness is not applicable; leading for equity involves adopting appropriate measures to support the learning of those with special needs. However, even in an equitable approach, the child or young person with special needs may still be seen as the 'problem'. The concept of inclusion goes one step further to place the onus on schools to adapt to the needs of the individual, whether students or staff. The over-riding term used in this book is 'equality', but in the case of special educational needs and disability, where there has been so much marginalization of individuals, the more appropriate concept may be 'inclusion'.

In this chapter we ask you to think about:

- what is meant by special/additional learning/educational needs, disability and inclusion
- current leadership challenges of the neo-liberal agenda and the demands of policy
- the role of the SENCo
- some of the strategies in leading for equality in special needs including:

    o working with external professionals
    o professional development for all staff

> o   the use of intervention
> o   deployment of support staff
> o   working with parents
> o   developing an inclusive culture.

In this chapter, case examples are drawn from two co-educational schools: Blackberry Primary (5–11), a small Church of England voluntary aided village school in the east of England; and Darnall All-age Academy, in a city in the south of England.

Special learning needs and inclusion

There is not much agreement internationally on the boundaries of special educational needs or the policies to adopt, but there is one commonality: that children with special educational needs and/or disabilities tend to be marginalized (Rix et al., 2012).

In England in 2014, 17.9 per cent of pupils were designated as having special educational needs (equating to 1,492,950 pupils) (DfE, 2014). Although children with the most severe needs constitute around 3 per cent of the population internationally, in the UK we tend to include a higher proportion of children who have less severe needs than other countries (Hartley, 2010). In the UK, a child or young person has special learning needs when learning is significantly more difficult than it would be for others of their age. In most cases, but not all, special needs also includes children whose disability prevents or hinders them from accessing the normal facilities provided in school. There are suggestions for additional reading on disability in children and teachers at the end but, since the principles of inclusion apply to both SEN and disability, this chapter focuses on special learning needs. Special educational needs are broadly defined under the following categories (Gov.uk, 2015):

- behaviour or ability to socialise, e.g. not being able to make friends
- reading and writing, e.g. they have dyslexia
- ability to understand things
- concentration levels, e.g. they have Attention Deficit Hyperactivity Disorder
- physical needs or impairments.

Additional learning needs (ALN) is a wider term that includes special needs. For example, in Wales in 2010 there were over 86,000 pupils on

ALN/SEN registers, but only 14,000 had statements of SEN (Estyn, 2013). These boundaries are not fixed in stone, and we might question why children from some backgrounds are so much more likely to be assessed as having special needs than others. For example, children with EAL may just need special support with language, yet are sometimes identified as having special needs. Equality issues and stereotyping have an effect on the assessment of special needs, and intersectionality with gender and ethnicity may come into play. For example, African-Caribbean boys are over-represented amongst pupils identified as having social and emotional difficulties (Frederickson and Cline, 2009). Schools do not always cope well with children with special needs. An indication is the fact that, in England, students with statements are seven times more likely than other pupils to be excluded from school on a permanent basis and nine times more likely to receive a fixed-term exclusion (DfE, 2012).

Over the years there have been major changes in our understanding of the concepts of special or additional learning/educational needs and disability.

Table 12.1 Changes in how special needs is seen

Special needs used to be seen as:	Now seen as:
A medical issue	A social or educational issue
A deficit of the individual	Requiring transformation of the school
Addressed outside the mainstream	Included in the mainstream

Right across the Western world there has been a move towards inclusion and the education of most children with special needs in mainstream rather than special schools (Terzi, 2008), but special schools are still the norm elsewhere, for example in India (Singal, 2010). In countries where school attendance is not universal, many children with special needs may not attend school at all. Despite the general move to the mainstream, special schools may actually give some children more equitable access to an education that suits their needs and, in England, over 100,000 children, or 0.8 per cent of the pupil population, attend special schools (Morrison, 2014). Norwich (2014) questions why a much greater proportion of children with special needs is educated in special schools during the secondary years than the primary years. A partial answer to this question may lie in the next section of the chapter which deals with conflicting agendas that particularly affect secondary school leaders.

Current leadership challenges

Conflicting agendas

In the UK and elsewhere there is a tension between the neo-liberal agenda of standards and league tables, and the inclusion of pupils with special needs. This potential for conflict has become an issue of real concern for leaders and governors in schools. It also raises the question of the purpose of education. Is it about narrow measures of attainment in examinations or about preparing a whole person to achieve their potential in life?

In a report for the NUT, Galton and MacBeath (2015) showed that in England the greatest concern of schools, in relation to inclusion of children with special needs, was clashes with the standards agenda and that their academic reputation, and Ofsted and league table ratings, would be damaged if they had a number of children with special educational needs. They also feared that having SEN children in the school might drive away parents with academic aspirations for their children. There are reports that the trend towards inclusion in the mainstream is now actually reversing because of this concern (Morrison, 2014).

In contrast, studies have shown that the proportion of children with SEN in a school does not necessarily have a negative effect on overall academic achievement, and that the measures taken to meet the needs of children with special needs are the same strategies that improve the learning of all pupils (Frederickson and Cline, 2009: 27). These strategies include having high quality specialist teachers, and especially taking an individual approach to each pupil, personalizing learning, and ensuring the careful monitoring and analysis of data relating to individual pupil progress (Ofsted, 2006). In addition, Thompson (2012) points out that supportive and collaborative practice helps to make a school both more inclusive and more effective. We will look further at these strategies later in the chapter.

Another conflict centres on the employment of disabled staff. Lepkowska (2012) reports that less than 1 per cent of teachers are disabled and that the proportion is likely to fall as schools' budgets decrease and they want to avoid the extra expenditure that might be necessary in supporting a teacher with disabilities.

Changing policy and the role of the SENCo

This example is specific to England, but shows how continuing changes in policy place demands on the leadership of schools in relation to SEN. The new Code of Practice for Special Educational Needs (DfE, 2015d) has brought about changes, amongst which are that it:

- covers a wider age range of 0–25 years
- stresses that views of children, young people and their families should be taken into account in planning for their future
- replaces statements of educational need with an Education, Health and Care (EHC) plan
- enhances the leadership role of the Special Educational Needs Coordinator (SENCo)
- requires the SENCo to obtain a leadership qualification.

In the case example that follows, the head teacher is also the SENCo. She identified the challenges she faced in relation to the introduction of the new Code:

Blackberry: the new Code

At present, the biggest challenge is getting the paperwork in order. This is partly the timing with the new assessment regime. In the guidance that I have been given the thresholds of need are all at the old levels and not yet converted, but the thresholds have been raised. My biggest frustration is finding ways of working with the thresholds to include children who I know need support.

I am also frustrated in that I understand how the One Planning process is a good idea, but we were doing that anyway. We were involving parents. It feels like we are just re-inventing. I must say our children are getting very good support, it is just the paperwork. It is arduous.

We can be creative because we are small. There are opportunities for a sort of cross-pollination of ideas as I am the SENCo as well as the head.

For a small school with clear and flexible ways of working, a change in practice can feel like an imposition and for all schools, small and large, there is a danger that the bureaucracy and form-filling associated with the role may dominate the SENCo's work. In contrasting the way that two SENCos work, Liasidou and Svensson (2012: 41) show how the role can be interpreted very differently. Both the SENCos were conscientious and hard-working, yet in one case 'her potential for driving the inclusion agenda was compromised because of the micro and bureaucratic nature of her tasks and her status'. In contrast, the other SENCo 'adopts a proactive strategic management role' and in this role she: nurtures a whole-school approach to inclusion; supports and mentors staff; facilitates new developments;

and is a member of the senior leadership team. In many schools, there is a need to transform the role of the SENCo from one that is bogged down in minutiae to one that is inspirational for all members of the community.

Strategies in leading for equality in special needs in schools

Aiming to achieve the best possible outcomes for pupils with special educational needs, schools can take a range of approaches on the best use of resources, human and financial. However, decisions will also depend on their local circumstances, and the number and type of additional educational needs in the school.

Working with external professionals

Depending on the types of need in the school, SENCos and others might routinely communicate with a wide variety of professionals. An educational psychologist working in the Greater London area who was interviewed for this chapter commented:

> There is also the challenge of SENCos having to juggle with all the different professionals they have to work with: speech and language therapists; occupational therapists; physiotherapists; sometimes teachers of the blind and the deaf; and school improvement teams from the local authority.

Dealing with so many different agencies was one of the problematic issues reported by Galton and MacBeath (2015). Managing a multi-disciplinary team concerned with the needs of one individual can be challenging. Coming from different specialisms, experts might have a range of beliefs, practices and terminology. Their funding might come from quite different sources. There may be practical and logistical difficulties in setting up meetings or common professional development at times and places suitable for all. Staff turnover may also be a problem. It is a challenge to leadership to find ways of working successfully together, ensuring there is sufficient time for meetings and establishing common ways of working together, including an efficient communication system and joint training, whilst making sure the needs of the child remain central. Ensuring that the SENCo has senior leadership status within the school is likely to be helpful.

However, the reduction in the services provided by the local authorities and the increasing expectation that funding will be located within schools in England have meant that there may be a case for minimizing the use of external professionals and instead developing in-house expertise. Later in the chapter you will read about the strategies adopted by the SENCo in an all-age academy. Here, she tells us about how little she employs external professionals:

Darnall: in-house expertise

We do [use external professionals] for some speech and language, but would like that to be in-house as well. We use an educational psychologist [EP] to a small extent. She has done one assessment for us this year but we are going to advertise for our own EP. Generally we have what we need in-house. Educational psychologists are rare. We had one severely dyslexic pupil and needed an EP report. It takes a long time for an EP to come in as they have a huge caseload. It gets very frustrating.

Whether expertise comes from outside the school or is located in-house, as we have already noted, there are considerable responsibilities of co-ordination and leadership vested in the SENCo, in order to ensure equality and inclusion for students with special needs.

Professional development

The potential for developing in-house expertise is limited by the time and the resources available but, for a school working towards inclusion, whole-school professional development is needed. A common vision has to be developed, with opportunities for all teachers to examine their own values and practice critically, as in the model offered in Chapter 11. The move towards including more children with special needs in mainstream schools, together with the fact that approaching 20 per cent of children may have some level of special need, indicates the necessity for all teachers to engage with appropriate professional development. As well as building a common vision of social justice and inclusion, professional development should ensure that teachers have enough actual knowledge about SEN to enable them to develop the practical tools and pedagogical skills to use in the classroom (Florian and Rouse, 2010).

It is important that individual teachers are empowered to work with all children in the classroom, rather than feeling that they are the responsibility of the special needs specialist. Obviously, the SENCo can support them, but all teachers should adopt and develop a reflective approach as they focus on the learning of the individual child, rather than on their disabilities. One of the two biggest challenges identified by SENCos taking part in the new leadership training in England was that of changing teachers' attitudes towards the teaching of children with SEN (Brown and Doveston, 2014). Continuing professional development for the SENCo is essential, particularly in relation to the leadership dimension of their role. Ideally, there would also be professional development for the governing body, particularly the member identified as having responsibility for special educational needs in the school (Pearson, 2010).

The use of interventions and the deployment of staff

One way in which SENCos can exert their leadership role and support the work of all teachers is through involving them in the strategic use of interventions and the way they deploy support staff. There has been some criticism of the effective use of teaching/learning support assistants in schools in England and Wales. The Deployment and Impact of Support Staff project found that the use of support staff for children with SEN tends to have a negative impact on the academic progress of the children. This seems to be because the teaching of the children is being left to the support person, who may be more concerned with the completion of tasks than the child's learning, so that in some cases the child is effectively being cut off from the learning experience in the classroom (Webster and Blatchford, 2015).

As part of the overall strategy in the case example that follows, the SENCo and the senior leadership team reviewed the way in which dedicated staff might best be deployed to be most effective. The SENCo has taken a radical stance on her use of learning support assistants in the school:

Darnall: deployment of staff for SEN

Senior leadership team:

> The SENCo is a member of the senior leadership team and an assistant head of school, but her main focus is on her special needs role.

(Continued)

(Continued)

In addition, she maintains her subject interest through ten hours of teaching each week. She has two assistant heads working directly to her, one for the Learning Zone (special needs area), who line manages the secondary learning support assistants, and one in charge of interventions across the whole school, who line manages the primary learning support assistants. There is also an assessment coordinator who is in charge of exams as well, and a life skills and nurture group coordinator who is responsible for running those groups and measuring their impact.

SENCo:

As SENCo I found that having learning support assistants in classrooms was not the main use I wanted to put them to. Their lack of in-depth subject knowledge can be an issue, and they were often being used to control behaviour in the classroom rather than support learning. We mainly use learning support assistants by attaching them to a faculty and they then offer support for the C/D borderline students in Key Stage 4.

Darnall School has adopted a strategy with regard to inclusion and special needs that is appropriate to its status and its particular pupil intake. About 150 pupils are designated as having additional educational needs, although very few have statements or EHC plans.

The main approach is for monitored interventions, where children are tested at the start and then re-tested, normally after six weeks. The careful collection and monitoring of data is vital to their approach:

Darnall: interventions

In terms of inclusion there has been a change in attitude with regard to support and intervention. We identify children with special educational needs early and personalize interventions according to needs. Sometimes six weeks of an intervention lead to an increase of two years of achievement, and they can access the curriculum and it minimizes low-level poor behaviour. Data are the key to it all.

We have the Learning Zone which is open all week. We extract students from class for individual or small group support for six weeks initially but the full time span is flexible. We get information from teachers and observe learners in class and then decide whether to continue or not. We have a wealth of resources now, but it has been a challenge prior to having the resources. We found that in-class support was not having the impact and that withdrawal interventions are more useful.

We run a range of individual programmes and interventions most of which last six weeks.

- Talking Partners is designed for children with communication difficulties, often with EAL. It is a ten-week programme.
- Mastering Memory is for short-term memory difficulties, three 20-minute sessions a week.
- Motor Skills United is for children with dyspraxia.
- There are one-to-one programmes of three 20-minute sessions a week for handwriting, spelling, reading skills and reading comprehension.
- A nurture group in Years 1 and 2.
- Life skills (a nurture group) in Year 7.
- Boys' group, designed for under-achieving boys in Years 7 and 8, running for three sessions a week, is a mixture of a nurture group and support for academic subjects.
- Boys' homework group, set up in reaction to boys not handing in homework, meets as a club twice a week after school and is compulsory. It operates mostly with Years 7 and 8.

In addition, the Learning Zone can be used flexibly depending on the need of the child: it could be support for EAL, maths or literacy, and sometimes Key Stage 4 children might need support to catch up on coursework or support with exams.

The children love the Learning Zone and it is an integral part of the school.

The careful monitoring of pupil progress, with extensive use of data, as mentioned above, is also the key to another aspect of the work with special educational needs; that of personalized learning. This demonstrates how classroom teachers are involved and supported by the SENCo:

Darnall: personalized learning

A big issue in the past was that there was no indication of the primary need of the children who might just be labelled as having moderate learning difficulties (MLD) for example. I looked at how to minimize these difficulties and I now use a number of assessment tools to assess the needs of the learners. For example, I might pinpoint comprehension as an issue for a particular child. I then give teachers strategies and resources to help support them. This has made our practice a lot easier. It is really personalized learning.

We have introduced Learning Portraits which are about the children and are completed after the child has had two sessions with one member of staff. It includes 'Interesting things about me', 'What am I good at?' 'What can I do to help myself?' 'What do I find difficult?' The information goes to all the teachers of the child. The folder also includes 'Strategies to help me succeed.' In addition to the folder the child can carry with them a laminated card that they can choose to put on their desk if they wish in each lesson so that the teacher can see the strategies that the child needs. Each Learning Portrait has a back sheet monitoring the progress of the child.

Finally, another aspect of Darnall School's strategy on special needs is involving parents:

Darnall: involving parents

Learning Portraits go home to parents, asking them what strategies work at home so that we can support them. Whenever a child is involved in an intervention a letter goes home to parents explaining the nature of the intervention and why their child is involved, and at the end they get a certificate indicating the level of progress.

Parents are invited into coffee mornings for the nurture group and then after eight weeks they are invited again and then again at the end of the intervention. When we have parents' consultation evenings they are invited to come in to the Learning Zone and have an informal chat.

The school in this example has been in existence in its present form for only a short time, so strategies are being evaluated and amended all the time. However, there are elements of good practice evident here that are widely endorsed in leading for SEN inclusion in schools. These include: the SENCo having senior leadership status; the use of personalized learning plans; careful data-driven monitoring of each student's progress involving classroom teachers; the structured but flexible use of learning support assistants; and, overall, an inclusive ethos in the school that involves parents, and where both students and parents see the Learning Zone as integral to the school and somewhere that they want to be.

The final case example comes from Blackberry School. The small size of the school means that its practice is different, but it is driven by the same issues that we have seen exemplified in the large all-age academy. In the example that follows the head teacher commented on how the school evaluates and judges its success, and on its approach to personalized learning:

Blackberry: evaluation

We get feedback through the SEN system. Behaviour Support [the team in the local authority] used one of our examples as a case study. They have said it is the most successful story we have had and we get lots of positive feedback. It is a small school and I am the head and the SENCo and I can make sure things happen in the way that a one day a week SENCo would not be able to. We also get family feedback pro formas now through the planning process. Every two years we give a general questionnaire to parents and of course we operate an open door policy. In terms of the children progressing we have our half-term reviews. Because of the way we work, two-thirds of the school have some kind of tweaking to their curriculum provision.

Following this example through, an ideal position might be adopting a personalized learning approach to all children, not just those with special or additional needs. The SEN label then becomes somewhat irrelevant. The focus is not on the children as a 'problem', but on the challenge of making teaching appropriate for all.

All schools have particular circumstances of location, intake, structure and history that will affect the approach they adopt. However, we feel that the following few key actions are probably generic for all schools.

Key actions

- Develop personalized learning for all, backed up by good data systems to ensure that education is effective for all pupils.
- Develop the ethos of the school so that an understanding of inclusion and equality for those with special needs or disability infuses the whole school community, including parents and governors.
- Ensure that all staff have access to relevant professional development, related to attitudes, knowledge and skills.
- Make leadership, not bureaucracy, the main focus of the work of the SENCo, who should be included as a member of the senior leadership team.
- Evaluate how strategies are working and be prepared to change.

For reflection and discussion

In relation to special/additional educational needs and disability, how do staff, governors and parents understand the concept of inclusion, as defined in Chapter 1? Would the strategies outlined at Darnall School be appropriate at your school?

Additional reading

If you are developing a vision for education for special educational needs, the following might be helpful:

Norwich, B. (ed.) (2014) 'A school for the future – 2025: practical futures thinking', *Journal of Research in Special Educational Needs*, 14 (1): 51–65.

For a more theoretical and philosophical approach:

Terzi, L. (2008) *Justice and Equality in Education*. London: Continuum.

For more about disabled teachers and staff:

NUT toolbag for supporting disabled teachers. www.teachers.org.uk/files/active/0/toolbag.pdf (accessed 05.05.16).
TUC (2015) *Disabled Workers and Students in Education*. London: TUC.

For an insight into the views of disabled students in mainstream schools:

Vlachou, A. and Papananou, I. (2015) 'Disabled students' narratives about their schooling experiences', *Disability & Society*, 30 (1): 73–86.

The impact of the inclusion of disabled students into mainstream schools is documented in:

Cairns, B. and McClatchey, K. (2013) 'Comparing children's attitudes towards disability', *British Journal of Special Education*, 40: 3.

The following books give more details on leading for inclusion and special educational needs:

Cornwall, J. and Graham-Matheson, L. (eds) (2011) *Leading on Inclusion: Dilemmas, Debates and New Perspectives*. London: Routledge.
Rose, R. (ed.) (2010) *Confronting Obstacles to Inclusion*. London: Routledge.

An overview of the European context is given in:

European Agency for Development in Special Needs Education (2013) *Organisation of Provision to Support Inclusive Education*. www.european-agency.org/agency-projects/organisation-of-provision (accessed 05.05.16).

Part III

Drawing together threads for action

13

Bringing it all together: Values, ethos, actions

Hope for each child's safe, happy and productive future depends on education. This is true for all, but especially for those whose background or characteristics mean they face a tougher journey. We trust that the previous chapters have left you in no doubt that education can fulfil such hope and act as a driver for greater equality, even though it does not always do so. This final chapter draws ideas together and focuses on the key lessons that have emerged. The area of equality is fraught with slippery language and paradox, so a simplistic 'one size fits all' action plan is not possible. Rather, we review the earlier discussion and illustrations to help you move towards your own judgements about the right goals and actions, in your context.

> In this chapter we ask you to think about:
>
> • why equality is important for all learners
> • maintaining a supportive ethos in current contexts
> • building capacity
> • forging goals and actions.

As this is the final chapter, to draw threads together we refer to quite a number of the case example schools used throughout this book. Illustrations are drawn from the community schools Allenridge (11–18), Maclear and Elands (both 11–16), Winburg Academy (11–18) and St Mary's Catholic School (11–16), all in the south of England; Glentanna Community Primary

(5–11) in Scotland; and Trichard Community Infants (5–7) in London. All are co-educational schools.

Equality matters

Our focus in Part II of the book is on groups of children with particular characteristics who may be at a disadvantage, and what action a school might take to offer them a fair education. We would not wish this to obscure the fact that equality matters a great deal to all children, including the privileged. The head teacher of Allenridge School stressed that many parents are well aware that their children's economic and emotional security is bound up with learning the values and skills offered by a school that puts equality at the core:

Allenridge: appropriate education for the twenty-first century

We make a strong pitch to parents. We say, 'if you want a good academic education go to any school in the area, but your children will be living and working in the cosmopolitan centres of large towns and cities. If you want them to have an edge, if you want them to have the skills and sensitivities to thrive in a multicultural setting, then send them to us and we will give them that edge'. There are over 50 languages spoken in the school. We celebrate other cultures and tell people's stories and we have a group of parents on the liberal left who want that for their children.

The head teacher of Maclear School makes a similar point: if children are to be fitted for twenty-first-century society, they need to learn a particular set of values, and this aspect of education is at least as valuable for their future as creditable examination outcomes:

Maclear: a microcosm of society

It's very much about recognizing that we're a microcosm of a multicultural society and we are an example where we respect everybody and try to meet the needs of children as much as you ever can. There is a real sense of care and kindness and respect.

Parents clearly value this oasis of respect, which is unlike what they generally experience. The curriculum director at Maclear recounted one parent's description of the school as something of a refuge, where different standards from those in the outside world could be counted on:

Maclear: a microcosm of society – a parent's view

It's almost like a bubble at Maclear because you're living that respect and courtesy and not the other end of racist stuff, but unfortunately what our students and our families experience outside is not of the same ilk.

This school offers children a chance to experience how a respectful society might function. The world outside the school may be different and harsher, but at least children are protected while in school, and can develop values and ideals to carry forward into their adult lives.

Striving for greater equality is impelled by arguments around human rights and justice, but it is also pragmatically in the interests of all children to learn to live in a diverse society, offering fairness and respect and expecting them in return. This foundational aspect of education has been advocated by the European Union ever more strongly in the light of a changing and often tense Europe: 'Ensuring inclusive education for all children and young people which combats racism and discrimination on any ground, promotes citizenship and teaches them to understand and to accept differences of opinion, of conviction, of belief and of lifestyle' (European Union, 2015c: 3).

Striving for greater equality is not only about giving the disadvantaged a fairer deal, but also about creating the society we want for us all.

The context

Two kinds of context can impact on schools' capacity to address inequality. The first is the national or regional policy context and the second the community context. The two are interconnected, as we have shown in Chapter 2. The policy context, with its emphasis on markets and choice, has increased competition and segregation between schools. The result is a widening division between schools with a majority of culturally and economically advantaged learners, and those where the socioeconomically or otherwise disadvantaged cluster. Nevertheless, many illustrations of practice in this book demonstrate that context need not determine outcomes. The policy context may create frustration and limitations, which we do not wish to minimize, nevertheless every school has a choice to accept the status quo or genuinely to push forward to make the system fairer. Looking across the chapters and the illustrations of practice, some themes emerge as critical in taking the latter path.

Ethos and culture

Despite the current context where there is a tendency to emphasize quantitative outcomes as measures of success, our case example schools are clear that achieving a certain kind of culture or ethos that embeds particular values is at least as important. As the head teacher of Winburg School explained, 'What is important is the impact, which is not always measurable – it is about ethos and harmony, and you can sense it when you go round the school'. The ethos is usually apparent to the school community and to those who visit, as in this example at St Mary's School:

St Mary's: ethos is felt, not measured

Well, I interviewed somebody the other day for a job and I thought they put it really neatly. My question was, 'What have you seen that would make you want to come and work here?' And they said, 'Oh it's nothing to do with what I've seen. It's what I feel'. And I thought that was it, in that answer, that was it. That is what is different about this school. It's what you feel when you walk in here rather than what you see that makes the difference.

Ethos is a tricky concept to define. It is discerned through observing, often unconsciously, the myriad daily choices made by individuals about how to act. Over time, those choices build an ethos that defines what and how it is acceptable to think and behave. Consequently, when sufficient staff and learners not only understand that, for example, bullying will not be tolerated, and also translate this into action by challenging bullying whenever they witness it, they change the ethos.

Because ethos is such a difficult concept to define and capture, some see it as a kind of soft option compared to using quantitative measures of outcomes. The illustrations of practice in this book show this to be far from the case. Ethos can be understood as allied to culture, which is highly resistant to change (Jenks, 1993; Lumby, 2012b; Lumby and Foskett, 2011). It is arguably far easier to shift examination results slightly each year than to change the underlying ethos of a school. Such a change implies moderating beliefs, attitudes and behaviour: a long-term and testing endeavour. Most schools have a statement of values, but if the words or actions that counter the values go unchallenged in the corridors, playground and classrooms, a different set of values and consequently ethos is present. Appropriate structures and policies are a good start, but if homophobic language or racist or religious rivalries, for example, are tacitly tolerated anywhere in the school, statements of equality in the prospectus and on the wall in the entry foyer are paper moons.

Several case examples stressed how many years it had taken to change the school ethos and how easy it is to let things slide back. For instance, Glentanna School determined that no child or member of staff should feel excluded because of their sexuality or that of their family. As discussed in Chapter 8, a range of initiatives began to dismantle heterosexual norms, but the bigger challenge was keeping the inclusive ethos alive on a permanent basis:

Glentanna: sustaining a changed ethos

We have now established this initiative and the current group of children know what the deal is. The challenge now is keeping it to the forefront, keeping everyone up to date and informed. There is a box of books that teachers can access, but we need to remind them, and keep it all alive.

An ethos that embodies particular values such as inclusion also implies tackling difficult challenges. In the case example that follows, Winburg School goes further than other local schools to make an inclusive ethos the school's reality:

Winburg: making an inclusive ethos reality

An issue arose in our area with two students who were tremendously physically disabled. One had no movement below the neck and the other had multiple problems including double incontinence. The parents

(Continued)

(Continued)

wanted them to be in mainstream. Other schools would not take them, but we made alterations and employed nursing staff. The parents were delighted and these children have had a positive impact on the rest of the school. It was a lot of work for us, but the disabled students themselves make such efforts that it has had a really good impact on others.

Establishing a fair and inclusive ethos is far from a soft option. It is built or dismantled by every choice that is taken, which children to enrol, what behaviour is acceptable, the nature of the curriculum and pedagogy; all must be assessed against the values of the school and, where they fall short, must be challenged.

Building capacity in staff, learners and parents

The ethos provides a framework within which goals can be set and actions assessed. More is needed, however, to build positive capacity: not just to eradicate attitudes and behaviour that run counter to the ethos but also to nurture knowledge and skills so that staff, learners and parents can together create support for all. 'Building capacity' is such an easy phrase to write, but the evidence presented in previous chapters suggests that schools all too often fall short. We have suggested that there are over-optimistic assumptions about teachers' mindset: their values, expectations and lack of prejudice. Building capacity is a major long-term undertaking that is not about criticizing individuals. It is about acknowledging and addressing thinking and attitudes that, however unconsciously, position the individual's assumptions as a norm against which everything else is measured. It is about challenging everyone.

Staff professional development

Staff may have had relatively little training in equality issues before entering the profession and few opportunities since. The starting point is therefore teachers' habitual ways of acting, which are shaped by their observation of colleagues and in order to survive. The experience of the head teacher of Glentanna School is that teachers will persist in their habitual ways of doing things unless asked to think critically about their practice. Just as children may adopt habits, for example, of using homophobic terms as part of their daily language and need to be challenged, so staff may unthinkingly carry forward attitudes that are translated into practice that excludes:

Glentanna: challenging sexist attitudes

Sometimes even teachers are not aware. Sometimes you have to educate teachers as well. They have done things a certain way over a long time and it is difficult to change. Maybe they do not think about equality. For example, we have just had a nativity. Teachers will be choosing girls to be an angel and boys to be a shepherd. We need to challenge and say that boys can be angels and girls can be shepherds.

Twenty years ago in teacher education it was a choice to do a course in equality. Now everyone should be thinking about it, but people don't see the bigger picture unless they are challenged.

Organizing appropriate development is not always easy. One-off workshops may be stimulating and enjoyable, but often do not have a long-term effect on practice (Guskey, 2002). Rather, what is needed is set out in Kutner's (1992) principles in Chapter 11. Staff need to work collaboratively to develop practice over time and will require a good deal of support in the long term. The head teacher of Winburg School initially found such support from outside agencies, but the long-term goal was to nurture sufficient knowledge and skill internally, to move to a self-sustaining development system:

Winburg: building development capacity

It is important to build capacity within the organization itself. In the early days we relied a lot on outside agencies. I think it is OK to do that at the start and then to work towards staff training staff and students working with students. Also I had a good chair of governors and not all governing bodies are that supportive. I have not heard many governing bodies talking seriously about equality. Local authorities have been weakened and schools need to look for support from elsewhere.

Across the case schools are multiple instances of training and development targeting particular aspects of inequality such as sexuality, racism, the under-representation of women or BME staff in leadership and so on. While this can achieve a great deal, it is not likely to be 100 per cent successful. It may be that some staff are unwilling to change their practice, or have deep-seated attitudes that cannot be adjusted. Ollis (2010) writes of only partial success in changing exclusionary attitudes to sexuality through development programmes. Where staff cannot align to the ethos of the school, despite support and development, the head teachers of Winburg and Maclear schools adopt the strategy of helping those staff to move on.

Approaches to building capacity

Chapter 5 discussed three approaches to increasing equality: a recognition or cultural approach, which focuses on better supporting marginalized groups; relational or participatory justice, which equips learners to play a full part in social relations and in society more broadly; and distributive justice, which allocates resources to 'level the playing field'. As argued in the chapter, a single strategy is unlikely to bring about sustainable change: the three broad strategies work together and can provide a framework for approaching professional development.

Recognition or cultural approach

Professional development that focuses on specific marginalized groups reflects a recognition or cultural approach, and is concerned to equip staff better to support children who are disadvantaged because of a special need or because they are seen as 'other' in some way. It is often the case that those staff who are most committed and knowledgeable about particular issues, such as homophobia or Islamophobia, are drawing on personal characteristics or experience. The majority will be less knowledgeable and likely to have a commitment to change that ranges from moderate to negligible. Professional development is needed to attack two angles: building commitment to change, and providing the knowledge and skills to translate commitment into action.

Participatory justice

Professional development is also needed to enable staff to work towards participatory justice. This has two aims: to ensure all learners are equipped to achieve in the system as it is; and to enable learners to be sufficiently confident and articulate to challenge it. Changing beliefs about the abilities and potential of all learners is one development aim. Developing skills of pedagogy, so that teaching engages and develops all to reach at least a minimum threshold, builds on this foundation. Development of curriculum and pedagogy to increase criticality in learners and the ability to articulate a point of view is a further aim for staff of all disciplines.

Distributive justice

Finally, distributive justice may be primarily about shifting resources to even up the playing field, but implies professional development needs. For example, if experienced staff have habitually taught high-level, high-attaining classes, they will need development if they are reallocated to spend part of their time with groups that, to date, have attained less. Additional resources offered to those students most in need, such as mentoring, will be effective only if the mentoring is of an appropriate quality, which again requires appropriate professional development.

In the case example schools we can see various approaches being used in tandem. There are illustrations not only of development related to meeting the needs of specific disadvantaged groups, such as working-class boys or migrant children, but also of across-the-board development to ensure that all learners meet threshold standards of achievement, so that they can look forward to taking a positive place in society. Though such developments may be shaped to help learners who are predicted to fall short of threshold standards, they are likely to raise achievement for all and be beneficial to the entire school. An appropriate curriculum and effective assessment, engaging teaching and personalized learning, all of which are designed to be inclusive, are good for high-attaining as well as struggling learners. Taking such a participatory approach is highly demanding of staff and requires considerable support.

Maclear School provided an example of the kind of challenge to be addressed through professional development:

Maclear: staff development for inclusion

Staff have received a lot of continuous professional development around that [building on individualized assessment] so every year we

(Continued)

(Continued)

re-address this and the teaching strategies, so every teacher has this as part of their planning tools and there have been challenges. It takes a lot of planning and a lot of differentiation and a lot of support EAL team working with those teachers.

I think its hugely demanding. Every time I see that list on a Friday I think somebody's going to have another student arrive at their classroom on Monday and there will be an additional person to try and cater for. So I think it's absolutely huge. It is a big ask but staff here are really committed to the students.

To meet this challenge, a framework for professional development using three approaches is suggested in Table 13.1.

Table 13.1 Approaches to staff development to increase equality

Approach to increasing equality	Aims	Examples of professional development
Recognition or cultural approach	To acknowledge the disadvantage experienced by learners in stigmatized or marginalized groups	Support for development of teaching plans and materials which shift the school away from White, heteronormative, Christian norms
	To embed a range of beliefs and experience in the school ethos, curriculum and pedagogy, steering away from a White Eurocentric norm	Leadership development for BME staff
Participatory justice	To ensure all learners achieve minimum standards of attainment	Support for development of inclusive pedagogies
	To equip learners to challenge inequalities while at school and in their adult life	Professional development for staff of all subject disciplines concerning language development for EAL learners
		Professional development to aid staff to embed development of critical thinking and effective communication skills across the curriculum
		Professional development in intercultural education supporting staff to develop learners' understanding of in-groups and out-groups
Distributive justice	To ensure resources are allocated effectively to offset the relative advantage of particular learners or learner groups	Professional development of mentors
		Professional development for teaching mixed ability groups

Table 13.1 provides only indicative examples of the kind of professional development that may be needed. The main point is the framework itself, with a focus on three different facets of equality. There is, of course, no neat division between the development aimed at each. The key argument is that in looking at a school's long-term plans to build capacity, a sophisticated analysis is required of how inequality is embedded in the school to underpin a long-term development plan.

Building learners' capacity

Building learners' capacity to challenge and to bring about change runs in parallel to staff development. In Chapters 2 and 5 we explored offering learners 'a *curriculum of access* and a *curriculum of dissent*' (Flecha, 2011: 8) so that they can both benefit from existing society and acquire tools to change it for the better. We have argued that a foundation is building confidence in children and young people. We have provided examples of schools located in communities of deep poverty, in towns and cities, and in rural locations, all of which refuse to accept any reason why they should not hold high expectations for all their learners, and use the curriculum both to support attainment and to develop social capital through acquiring values and skills.

Just as ethos needs to be embedded in a daily insistence on particular standards of behaviour, so high expectations and confidence in children need to be demonstrated and enacted in concrete ways, as illustrated in Chapter 8. When Glentanna School wished to ensure all its staff and children felt equally included, whatever their sexuality or that of their parents, the children were given a key role. It was the children who ran an information booth on the sexuality work at the school on parents' evening, and children who approached the local education authority to push their practice forward on a wider front. Building confidence in children implies trusting their abilities.

Our case examples also 'look at how the curriculum works to develop values across the board' (Allenridge School). Rather than a discrete one-off session or module on an equality-related issue, our case examples stress adjusting the curriculum holistically. Allenridge, for example, does not merely cover sexuality equality in its personal and social education – it embeds it: 'One of the key things is joining up every aspect of the school's work and not just looking at sexuality in isolation. For example look at the link with citizenship, with English and with science, with all the subjects'. Equality relating to sexuality is just one example. Ensuring the curriculum allows students to reach threshold standards of achievement, and to develop skills to be critically aware of where that curriculum comes from and to dissent in respectful and tolerant ways, comprises the dual ongoing challenge to build capacity in learners and achieve greater equity, as defined in Chapter 5.

Building parents' capacity

The history of relations between teachers and parents is outlined by Vincent (2013). Parents have been often been viewed as external to the school, their role to offer support for what the school decides to do. They are sometimes judged negatively as a toxic influence on their children's lives that needs to be countered by the alternative values and behaviour within the school. Well-used stereotypes such as the pushy middle-class mother or the aggressive working-class father regularly surface.

Within our case example schools there are certainly narratives of angry or aggressive parents. The response has been to recognize an underlying trigger in the quite reasonable fear of some parents that the school will not offer their children a fair chance, especially when that child comes from, for example, a socioeconomically disadvantaged background or is a migrant or has some other stigmatized characteristic. For example, Wilkin et al. (2010) state that the Traveller community often think that schools harm their children:

Elands: aggressive parents

We have some aggressive parents. We have some parents who open their mouth before they really think, but they are fundamentally hard-working people that want the best for their children. I think what we have had to do in the last four years is to prove to them that we are on their side. We're going to do it slightly differently without kind of antagonizing them by saying 'we are the professionals let us do our job' and alienating them. It's saying 'work with us and we'll have some differences along the way, but be under no illusion we are on your side and we want the best for your child'. I think that's a different type of conversation we would be having with parents.

The impact of that is we get more parental engagement in the school, more parents come to parents' evenings. More parents will come in if they've got an issue or complaints, but I don't get many complaints. I am likely to get issues/queries about homework not being marked or not being set rather that disruption and disruptive behaviour in the school. So in terms of culture we are kind of moving it in the right direction.

Those are the kinds of conversations that are now going on and we find that the relationships with parents are much more cordial, much more friendly. They might still ring up and shout and swear down the phone at us, but once you've convinced parents that you are doing the right thing they are very supportive.

Maclear School faces a different kind of challenge in that it has parents from many different parts of the world whose culture, experience and expectations of education may vary widely:

Maclear: parents' experience of education

I think parents are a bigger challenge. Their experiences of education in the countries they've come from can be very different, so some will have had a very high level of education and some no education at all, and I think working with the parents to help them understand our education system and how different it is is a challenge our staff face.

The Somali community is significant here ... I used to get deputations, groups of parents that came in and shouted at me to tell me how to do things. We've moved a long way from that. I think primarily it's the students, because it's the students who are completely onside and are happy and doing well and so all of that drops away. Our attendance at parents' evenings ... A lot of parents live right down in the city and transport in this city, like many others, is not easy or straightforward. We get between 60 per cent and 70 per cent, which is much higher than it's been. We've been watching it go up.

The key point in both of these case examples is that if children are doing well, parent aggression decreases and support increases. A second element is respect for parents. In both cases, staff recognize that many parents are dealing with difficult challenges and are deeply concerned for their children. As a consequence, they relate to parents with respect. An instance of this is at Maclear School, which is obliged to operate the national Prevent strategy concerned with averting radicalization of young people in schools.

Many of the parents are Muslim and feel stigmatized. Consequently, they were suspicious of the school's intentions. The issue was tackled head on:

Maclear: tackling difficult issues

The Prevent agenda for example could be highly contentious, very sensitive, but we took the decision that we weren't going to hide from it so we invited the local Prevent man who came in, talked to all the staff about exactly what it was all about and what our responsibilities are. Every year group had an assembly with him, so we're much more about being open, putting it out there and then taking questions, any issues that come up from individuals.

Then we went to the Parents' Voice, which is not the governors. It's a group of interested parents who can meet with us twice a term about all sorts of issues, usually at their direction to some extent. A question from one of the Muslim dads came up. He wanted to know what our stance was on this and we had quite a discussion about it, because again it is so sensitive and our view is absolutely that it's certainly not about the Islamic faith. It's about all extreme views and we talked at some length.

In all the examples related to building capacity in parents – that is, their understanding of the education system and faith in the school – it is the learners who are of key importance. They are the chief link with parents. If they are confident, working hard, achieving the best they can and feeling they have a positive stake in the school community, most of their parents become more open to communication and collaboration. If children feel excluded or unhappy, it is not surprising that angry parents choose either to voice their concerns or just stay away. There is no panacea for building positive relations with all parents, yet a recognition that meeting children's needs, and relating with respect to both children and parents, represents a more embedded approach to bringing parents on board than initiatives focusing merely on infrequent formal communication with parents, such as parents' evenings and newsletters.

Goals and actions

We hope that this book has provided a range of ideas about possible goals and the approaches to achieve them. As you formulate aims and strategy for your class, department, school or cluster of schools, the key actions and points for reflection and discussion at the end of each chapter can be used as a basis for school planning and professional development.

We have offered some key lessons about increasing equality. The first is the requirement for a dual focus, where schools must meet the needs of specific disadvantaged individuals or groups but, in doing so, improve things for everyone. It is not 'either/or', but both. Second, it is not just about attainment and outcomes. It is also about process. A negative experience of school is not recoverable. While some learners might go on to be more successful in education or training as adults, years when most of their waking hours at school are unhappy remain a blot on their lives, at best, and at worst can cause long-term social and psychological damage. Third, while statements and policies have their place, it is action – persistent action – that creates change. If all schools truly reflected the values stated on their classroom walls, this book would be unnecessary. What we say is always overpowered by what we do. The occasional gesture will not be enough. Consistent, persistent action in the long term is needed.

Finally, we need to stop locating the problem with learners themselves, with their families or with individual staff members. We are all caught up in a web of assumptions about learning and learners that works to disadvantage further those who start off with disadvantage. The 'Matthew effect', as explained in Chapter 1, is rarely intentional, but rather a result of the adoption of existing assumptions and patterns of behaviour. We need to support each other to bring about change rather than focus on deficit. The aim to increase equality is consequently likely to have multiple objectives, including ensuring that all learners reach a minimum threshold of attainment, that every child feels they have a respected place in the community, and that each acquires the skills and principles to enable them to live a life they value in a diverse twenty-first-century society. Most schools would say these are already their goals but, as we have argued throughout the book, it is not yet a reality for many learners.

Early on, in Chapter 2, we discussed evidence of failure of equality in schools. Writing this final chapter more than a year later, the situation has not improved significantly. The latest European Union education and training report concludes that 'Inequality is at its highest level in 30 years in most European and OECD countries' (European Union, 2015b: 10). Set against this bleak picture are the inspirational examples throughout the book of schools that are working to ensure that nobody feels excluded.

When asked how change had been brought about, the head teacher of Trichard School in London answered, 'through training, not being afraid of grasping the nettle and working on lots of fronts at the same time – in staffing appointments, by timetabling, by changing expectations'. Thinking through a long-term plan to increase equality requires deep understanding of the goals and a range of approaches and strategies to achieve them. Above all, it depends on the commitment and determination of staff to keep working at it. A more positive future may only ever be one generation away, but achieving it depends on the education of our children. Society's fundamental dependence on education is a challenge to our schools, at no time more so than in the twenty-first-century when societal and global changes threaten to destabilize our communities. Though the challenge may at times seem daunting, it is the greatest achievement of educators to contribute to a better future through our children.

Key actions

As we have stressed repeatedly, each school works in a specific context. The needs of its learners are paramount. Consequently, key actions should be shaped to accommodate particular contextual factors.

- Agree how equality is understood in the school and a range of objectives and strategies to achieve this, drawing on ideas in this book.
- Build the school ethos by persistently challenging any behaviour that contradicts the school values.
- Build capacity in staff, bearing in mind alternative approaches to achieving greater equality relating to recognition, participatory and distributive notions of justice.
- Investigate to what degree expectations of learners are influenced by irrelevant characteristics such as socioeconomic or migrant status. Work to make high expectations a reality through policies, structures and behaviour.
- Build capacity in learners by offering leadership opportunities and trusting their abilities, even though they may sometimes make mistakes.
- Communicate to parents persistently your concern for their children and respect for their position.
- Tackle sensitive issues such as anti-radicalization directly with staff, learners and parents.
- Give responsibility for scrutinizing monitoring data to a number of people, so that they can reflect and report on how progress is being made from a number of different perspectives.
- Keep going!

For reflection and discussion

Marshal and review evidence on your school's performance from the point of view of both process and outcomes. How successful is it in making the school a positive environment for all? How successful is it in supporting all learners to achieve their potential?

Additional reading

For ideas about why increasing equality is so important:

Wilkinson, R. and Pickett, K. (2009) *The Spirit Level: Why More Equal Societies Almost Always Do Better.* London: Allen Lane.

For narratives about individual leaders attempting to increase equality:

Encarnación, Garza Jr. (2008) 'Autoethnography of a first-time superintendent: challenges to leadership for social justice', *Journal of Latinos and Education,* 7 (2): 163–76.
Jansen, J. (2006) 'Leading against the grain: the politics and emotions of leading for social justice in South Africa', *Leadership and Policy in Schools,* 5 (1): 37–51.

For approaches to developing staff capacity:

Bruner, D.Y. (2008) 'Aspiring and practicing leaders addressing issues of diversity and social justice', *Race, Ethnicity and Education,* 11 (4): 483–500.
Florian, L. (2012) 'Preparing teachers to work in inclusive classrooms: key lessons for the professional development of teacher educators from Scotland's Inclusive Practice Project', *Journal of Teacher Education,* 63 (4): 275–85.
Rusch, E.A. and Douglass Horsford, S. (2008) 'Unifying messy communities: learning social justice in educational leadership classrooms', *Teacher Development: An International Journal of Teachers' Professional Development,* 12 (4): 353–67.

For approaches to developing student capacity:

Cook-Sather, A., Cohen, J. and Alter, Z. (2010) 'Students leading the way toward social justice within and beyond the classroom', *Equity & Excellence in Education,* 43 (2): 155–72.
Roberts, A. and Nash, J. (2009) 'Enabling students to participate in school improvement through a Students as Researchers programme', *Improving Schools,* 12 (2): 174–87.
Thomson, P. and Gunter, H. (2006) 'From "consulting pupils" to "pupils as researchers": a situated case narrative', *British Educational Research Journal,* 32 (6): 839–56.

For approaches to developing parent relations:

Hornby, G. and Lafaele, R. (2011) 'Barriers to parental involvement in education: an explanatory model', *Educational Review*, 63 (1): 37–52.

Hornby, G. and Witte, C. (2010) 'Parent involvement in rural elementary schools in New Zealand: a survey', *Journal of Child and Family Studies*, 19 (6): 771–7.

LaRocque, M., Kleiman, I. and Darling, S.M. (2011) 'Parental involvement: the missing link in school achievement', *Preventing School Failure*, 55 (3): 115–22.

Vincent, C. (2013) *Parents and Teachers: Power and Participation*. London: Routledge.

References

Abbott, I., Middlewood, D. and Robinson, S. (2015) 'It's not just about value for money: a case study of values-led implementation of the Pupil Premium in outstanding schools', *Management in Education*, 0892020615593789.

Abrams, F. (2011) 'Islamic schools flourish to meet demand', *The Guardian*, 28 November. www.theguardian.com/education/2011/nov/28/muslim-schools-growth (accessed 15.12.15).

Agirdag, O., Van Houtte, M. and Van Avermaet, P. (2012) 'Why does the ethnic and socioeconomic composition of schools influence math achievement? The role of sense of futility and futility culture', *European Sociological Review*, 28 (3): 366–78.

Ainscow, M. (2005) 'Developing inclusive education systems: what are the levers for change?', *Journal of Educational Change*, 6 (2): 109–24.

Ainscow, M., Dyson, A., Goldrick, S. and West, M. (2012) 'Making schools effective for all: rethinking the task', *School Leadership & Management: Formerly School Organisation*, 32 (3): 197–213.

Allen, R. and West, A. (2011) 'Why do faith secondary schools have advantaged intakes? The relative importance of neighbourhood characteristics, social background and religious identification amongst parents', *British Educational Research Journal*, 37 (4): 691–712.

Anderson, B. and Blinder, S. (2015) *Who Counts as a Migrant? Definitions and Their Consequences*. Oxford: University of Oxford. www.migrationobservatory.ox.ac.uk/sites/files/migobs/Briefing%20-%20Who%20Counts%20as%20a%20Migrant.pdf (accessed 17.11.15).

Andraos, M.E. (2012) 'Engaging diversity in teaching religion and theology: an intercultural, de-colonial epistemic perspective', *Teaching Theology and Religion*, 15 (1): 3–15.

Applebaum, B. (2008) '"Doesn't my experience count?" White students, the authority of experience and social justice pedagogy', *Race Ethnicity and Education*, 11 (4): 405–14.

Archer, L. and Francis, B. (2007) *Understanding Minority Ethnic Achievement*. Abingdon: Routledge.

Association of Muslim Schools (AMS) (2015) http://ams-uk.org/faq/ (accessed 03.02.15).

Bailey, R. (2009) 'Well-being, happiness and education', *British Journal of Sociology of Education*, 30 (6): 795–802.

Ball, S.J. (2003) *Class Strategies and the Education Market: The Middle Classes and Social Advantage*. London: Routledge.

Ball, S.J. (2006) *Education Policy and Social Class: The Selected Works of Stephen J. Ball*. Abingdon: Routledge.

Ball, S.J. and Youdell, D. (2008) *Hidden Privatisation in Public Education*. Brussels: Education International.

Batalova, J. and McHugh, M. (2010) *Number and Growth of Children in US Schools in Need of English Instruction*. ELL Fact Series. www.migrationpolicy.org/research/number-and-growth-students-us-schools-need-english-instruction (accessed 18.02.15).

Beach, D. and Dovemark, M. (2009) 'Making "right" choices? An ethnographic account of creativity, performativity and personalised learning policy, concepts and practices', *Oxford Review of Education*, 35 (6): 689–704.

Bennathan, M. and Boxall, M. (2010) *Effective Intervention in Primary School: Nurture Groups*, 2nd edn. Abingdon: Routledge.

Bhopal, K. (2012) 'Islam, education and inclusion: towards a social justice agenda?', *British Journal of Sociology of Education*, 33 (5): 783–90.

Blackmore, J. (2009) 'Leadership for social justice: a transnational dialogue', *Journal of Research on Leadership Education*, 4 (1): 1–10.

Blase, J. and Blase, J. (2004) 'The dark side of school leadership: implications for administrator preparation', *Leadership and Policy in Schools*, 3 (4): 245–73.

Bloem, N.S. and Diaz, R. (2007) 'White flight: integration through segregation in Danish metropolitan public schools', *Humanity in Action*, Team Denmark.

Bohlmark, A. and Lindahl, M. (2007) 'The impact of school choice on pupil achievement, segregation and costs: Swedish evidence', IZA Discussion Papers, No. 2786. www.econstor.eu/bitstream/10419/34645/1/555455319.pdf (accessed 27.11.15).

Bradbury, A. (2014) 'Identity, performance and race: the use of critical race theory in understanding institutional racism and discrimination in schools', in R. Race and V. Lander (eds), *Advancing Race and Ethnicity in Education*. Basingstoke: Palgrave Macmillan, pp. 17–31.

Brown, J. and Doveston, M. (2014) 'Short sprint or an endurance test: the perceived impact of the National Award for Special Educational Needs Coordination', *Teacher Development*, 18 (4): 495–510.

Bryant, E. (2015) 'French court rules school lunches may include pork; Muslims alarmed', *Religious News Service*. www.religionnews.com/2015/08/13/french-court-rules-school-lunches-may-include-pork-muslims-alarmed/ (accessed 27.10.15).

Bush, T., Glover, D. and Sood, K. (2006) 'Black and Minority Ethnic leaders in England: a portrait', *School Leadership and Management*, 26 (3): 289–305.

Campbell, R.J., Kyriakides, L., Muijs, R.D. and Robinson, W. (2003) 'Differential teacher effectiveness: towards a model for research and teacher appraisal', *Oxford Review of Education*, 29 (3): 347–62.

Campbell-Stephens, R. (2009) 'Investing in diversity: changing the face (and heart) of educational leadership', *School Leadership and Management*, 29 (3): 321–31.

Capper, C.A., Dantley, M., González, M.L., Bell McKenzie, N.K. Christman, D.E., Hernandez, F. and Fierro, E. (2007) 'From the field: a proposal for educating leaders for social justice', *Educational Administration Quarterly*, 44: 111.

Carrington, B., Tymms, P. and Merrell, C. (2008) 'Role models, school improvement and the 'gender gap': do men bring out the best in boys and women the best in girls?', *British Educational Research Journal*, 34 (3): 315–27.

Carrington, S., Mercer, K.L., Iyer, R. and Selva, G. (2015) 'The impact of transformative learning in a critical service-learning program on teacher development: building a foundation for inclusive teaching', *Reflective Practice*, 16 (1): 61–72.

Children's Society (2015) *The Good Childhood Report 2015*. www.childrenssociety. org.uk/sites/default/files/TheGoodChildhoodReport2015.pdf (accessed 15.11.15).

Clarke, L. and Winch, C. (eds) (2007) *Vocational Education: International Approaches, Developments and Systems*. London: Routledge.

Clarke, P. (2014) *Report into Allegations Concerning Birmingham Schools Arising from the 'Trojan Horse' Letter*. London: Department for Education.

Coleman, M. (2007) 'Gender and educational leadership in England: a comparison of secondary head teachers' views over time', *School Leadership and Management*, 2 (4): 383–99.

Commission for Developing Scotland's Young Workforce (2014) *Education Working for All! Final Report*. Edinburgh: Scottish Government.

'Compulsory Christian school assembly should be scrapped' (2015) 'Compulsory Christian school assembly should be scrapped – Church of England education chief', *Telegraph,* 9 December. www.telegraph.co.uk/education/education news/10951894/Compulsory-Christian-school-assembly-should-be-scrapped-Church-of-England-education-chief.html (accessed 09.12.15).

Copeland, W., Wolke, D., Angold, A. and Costello, E. (2013) 'Adult psychiatric outcomes of bullying and being bullied by peers in childhood and adolescence', *JAMA Psychiatry, 70* (4): 419–26.

Cork, L. (2005) *Supporting Black Pupils and Parents: Understanding and Improving Home–School Relations*. London: Routledge.

Coughlan, S. (2015) 'Primary school pupil numbers soaring', *BBC News*, 11 June. www.bbc.co.uk/news/education-33094304 (accessed 27.11.15).

Council on Foreign Relations (2015) *Europe's Migration Crisis*. www.cfr.org/migra tion/europes-migration-crisis/p32874 (accessed 27.11.15).

Creemers, B.P., Kyriakides, L. and Sammons, P. (2010) *Methodological Advances in Educational Effectiveness Research*. London: Routledge.

Crenshaw, K. (1989) 'Demarginalizing the intersection of race and sex: a Black feminist critique of antidiscrimination doctrine, feminist theory, and antiracist politics', *University of Chicago Legal Forum*, 1 (8): 139–67.

Croxford, L. (2001) 'School differences and social segregation: comparison between England, Wales and Scotland', *Education Review*, 15 (1): 68–73.

Crozier, G. (2014) 'Foreword', in R. Race and V. Lander, *Advancing Race and Ethnicity in Education*. Basingstoke: Palgrave Macmillan, pp. viii–xiii.

Dar, A. (2015) *Youth Unemployment Statistics 17 June 2015*. London: Houses of Parliament. http://researchbriefings.parliament.uk/ResearchBriefing/Summary/ SN05871 (accessed 14.06.15).

D'Arcy, K. (2014) 'Educational inclusion: meeting the needs of all Traveller pupils', in R. Race and V. Lander (eds), *Advancing Race and Ethnicity in Education*. Basingstoke: Palgrave Macmillan, pp. 47–62.

Darmody, M., Byrne D. and McGinnity, F. (2014) 'Cumulative disadvantage? Educational careers of migrant students in Irish secondary schools', *Race, Ethnicity and Education*, 17 (1): 129–51.

Davie, G. (2009) 'Christian, but not as we know it', *The Guardian*, 1 June. www.theguardian.com/commentisfree/belief/2009/jun/01/europe-christianity-religion (accessed 04.05.16).

DCSF (2007) *Homophobic Bullying: Safe to Learn – Embedding Anti-Bullying Work in Schools*. Nottingham: DCSF.

DCSF (2009) *Gender and Education: Mythbusters*. http://webarchive.national archives.gov.uk/20130401151715/http://www.education.gov.uk/publications/eOrderingDownload/00599-2009BKT-EN.pdf (accessed 15.08.15).

Delhaxhe, A. (2009) *Gender Differences in Educational Outcomes: Study on the Measures Taken and the Current Situation in Europe*. Brussels: Eurydice.

Denessen, E., Driessena, G. and Sleegers, P. (2005) 'Segregation by choice? A study of group-specific reasons for school choice', *Journal of Education Policy*, 20 (3): 347–68.

De Palma, R. and Atkinson, E. (2009) '"No outsiders": moving beyond a discourse of tolerance to challenge heteronormativity in primary schools', *British Educational Research Journal*, 35 (6): 837–55.

Devine, D. (2013) '"Value"ing children differently? Migrant children in education', *Children & Society*, 27 (4): 282–94.

DfE (2012) *A Profile of Pupil Exclusions in England*. www.gov.uk/government/uploads/system/uploads/attachment_data/file/183498/DFE-RR190.pdf (accessed 11.10.15).

DfE (2013) *Statistical First Release: Schools Pupils and Their Characteristics*, January. www.gov.uk/government/statistics/schools-pupils-and-their-character istics-january-2013 (accessed 04.05.16).

DfE (2014) *Statistical Release: Children with Special Educational Needs 2014: An Analysis*. www.gov.uk/government/collections/statistics-special-educationalneeds-sen (accessed 11.10.15).

DfE (2015a) *Statistical First Release, Pupil Absence in Schools in England: Autumn Term 2014*. London, DfE. www.gov.uk/government/uploads/system/uploads/attachment_data/file/428578/SFR12_2015_Text.pdf (accessed 05.01.16).

DfE (2015b) Statistical first release. NEET Quarterly Brief – April to June 2015. London: DfE. www.gov.uk/government/uploads/system/uploads/attachment_data/file/454401/Quarterly_Brief_NEET_Q2_2015.pdf (accessed 07.09.15).

DfE (2015c) *Statistical First Release: Schools Pupils and their Characteristics*, January. www.gov.uk/government/statistics/schools-pupils-and-their-character istics-january-2015 (accessed 11.10.15).

DfE (2015d) *Special Educational Needs and Disability Code of Practice: 0 to 25 Years*. London: DfE.

DfES (2005) *Higher Standards, Better Schools for All* (White Paper). London: HMSO.

Dinham, A. and Shaw, M. (2015) *REforREal Report: The Future of Teaching and Learning About Religion and Belief*. London: Culham St Gabriel's/Goldsmiths. www.gold.ac.uk/media/goldsmiths/169-images/departments/research-units/faiths-unit/REforREal-web-b.pdf (accessed 04.05.16).

Du Bois, W.E.B. (1903/1968) *The Souls of Black Folk*. New York: Johnson Reprint Company.

EHRC (2011) *Sex and Power 2011*. Manchester: Equality and Human Rights Commission.

Ellis, V. with High, S. (2004) 'Something more to tell you: gay, lesbian or bisexual young people's experiences of secondary schooling', *British Educational Research Journal*, 30 (2): 213–25.

Elton-Chalcraft, S. (2009) *'It's Not Just About Black and White, Miss': Children's Awareness of Race*. Stoke on Trent: Trentham Books.

Estyn (2013) *Supplementary Guidance: Additional Learning Needs*. Cardiff: Estyn.

European Agency for Development in Special Needs Education (2009) *Multicultural Diversity and Special Needs Education*. Denmark: European Agency for Development in Special Needs Education.

European Commission (2014) *Overview of Europe 2020 Targets*. Brussels: European Commission. http://ec.europa.eu/europe2020/pdf/targets_en.pdf (accessed 27.04.16).

European Migration Network (2011) *Annual Report on Migration and International Protection Statistics 2008*. Helsinki: EMN. http://emn.ie/files/p_2011111103371 42011_Synthesis_AR_Statistics2008_FINAL_October_2011.pdf (accessed 05.06.16).

European Union (2015a) Poverty and social exclusion. http://ec.europa.eu/social/ main.jsp?catId=751 (accessed 14.06.15).

European Union (2015b) *Declaration on Promoting Citizenship and the Common Values of Freedom, Tolerance and Non-discrimination through Education*. http://ec.europa.eu/education/news/2015/documents/citizenship-education-declaration_en.pdf (accessed 04.05.16).

European Union (2015c) *2015 Joint Report of the Council and the Commission on the Implementation of the Strategic Framework for European Cooperation in Education and Training*. Brussels: EU.

Eurostat (2015) Employment Statistics May. http://ec.europa.eu/eurostat/statistics-explained/index.php/Unemployment_statistics (accessed 14.06.15).

Eyles, A. and Machin, S. (2014) *The Introduction of Academy Schools to England's Education* (mimeo). London: Centre for Economic Performance.

Fair Education Alliance (2014) 'Will we ever have a fair education for all? The Fair Education Alliance Report Card 2014'. http://static1.squarespace.com/static/ 543e665de4b0fbb2b140b291/t/5481a731e4b0d2f5ad3b39fb/1417783096688/ FEA+Report+Card+2014.pdf (accessed 28.08.15).

Farkas, L. (2014) *Report on Discrimination of Roma Children in Education*. Brussels: EU. http://ec.europa.eu/justice/discrimination/files/roma_childdiscrimination_ en.pdf (accessed 12.11.15).

Fawcett Society (2015) *The Gender Pay Gap*. www.fawcettsociety.org.uk/our-work/ campaigns/gender-pay-gap/ (accessed 17.10.15).

Ferri, B.A. and Connor D.J. (2010) '"I was the special ed. girl": urban working-class young women of colour', *Gender and Education*, 22 (1): 105–21.

Field, S., Kuczera, M. and Pont, B. (2007) *No More Failures: Ten Steps to Equity in Education*. Summary and policy recommendations. Paris: OECD. www.oxydi ane.net/IMG/pdf/No_More_Failure.pdf (accessed 05.05.16).

Fitz, J., Davies, B. and Evans, J. (2005) *Education Policy and Social Reproduction: Class Inscription and Symbolic Control*. London: Routledge.

Flecha, R. (2011) 'The dialogic sociology of education', *International Studies in Sociology of Education*, 21 (1): 7–20.

Flint, J. (2007) 'Faith schools, multiculturalism and community cohesion: Muslim and Roman Catholic state schools in England and Scotland', *Policy & Politics*, 35 (2): 251–68.

Flintoff, A., Fitzgerald, H. and Scraton, S. (2008) 'The challenges of intersectionality: researching difference in physical education', *International Studies in Sociology of Education*, 18 (2): 73–85. http://eprints.leedsbeckett.ac.uk/363/1/Flintoffetal2 008IntStudiesinSocEducation.pdf (accessed 12.08.15).

Florian, L. and Linklater, H. (2010) 'Preparing teachers for inclusive education: using inclusive pedagogy to enhance teaching and learning for all', *Cambridge Journal of Education*, 40 (4): 369–86.

Florian, L. and Rouse, M. (2010) 'Teachers' professional learning and inclusive practice', in R. Rose (ed.), *Confronting Obstacles to Inclusion*. London: Routledge, pp. 185–200.

Foskett, N., Dyke, M. and Maringe, F. (2008) 'The influence of the school in the decision to participate in learning post-16', *British Educational Research Journal*, 34 (1): 37–61.

Foskett, N. and Lumby, J. (2003) *Leading and Managing Education: International Dimensions*. London: Paul Chapman.

Francis, B. (2006) 'The nature of gender', in C. Skelton, B. Francis and L. Smulyan (eds), *The Sage Handbook of Gender and Education*. London: Sage, pp. 7–17.

Francis, B., Skelton, C. and Read, B. (2010) 'The simultaneous production of educational achievement and popularity: how do some pupils accomplish it?' *British Educational Research Journal*, 36 (2): 317–40.

Francis, L.J., Pyke, A. and Penny, G. (2015) 'Christian affiliation, Christian practice, and attitudes to religious diversity: a quantitative analysis among 13- to 15-year-old female students in the UK', *Journal of Contemporary Religion*, 30 (2): 249–63.

Fraser, N. (1997) *Justice Interruptus: Critical Reflections on the 'Postsocialist' Condition*. New York: Routledge.

Frederickson, N. and Cline, T. (2009) *Special Educational Needs, Inclusion and Diversity*. Maidenhead: Open University Press.

Fuller, K. (2013) *Gender, Identity and Educational Leadership*. London: Bloomsbury.

Furman, G. (2012) 'Social justice leadership as praxis: developing capacities through preparation programs', *Educational Administration Quarterly*, 48 (2): 191–229. http://eaq.sagepub.com/content/early/2012/01/03/ 0013161X11427394

Furman, G. and Shields, C. (2005) 'How can educational leaders promote and support social justice and democratic community in schools?', in W.A. Firestone and C. Riehl (eds), *A New Agenda for Research in Educational Leadership*. New York: Teachers College Press, pp. 119–37.

Galton, M. and MacBeath, J. (2015) *Inclusion: Statements of Intent*. London: NUT.

Gamoran, A. (2001) 'American schooling and educational inequality: a forecast for the 21st century', *Sociology of Education* (Extra Issue): 135–53.

Gamoran, A. (2010) 'Tracking and inequality', in M. Apple, S. Ball and L.A. Gandin (eds), *The Routledge Handbook of the Sociology of Education*. London: Routledge, pp. 213–28.

Gewirtz, S. and Cribb, A. (2002) 'Plural conceptions of social justice: implications for policy sociology', *Journal of Education Policy*, 17 (5): 499–509.

Gibbons, S., Machin, S. and Silva, O. (2008) 'Choice, competition, and pupil achievement', *Journal of the European Economic Association*, 6 (4): 912–47.

Gillborn, D. (2010) 'The white working class, racism and respectability: victims, degenerates and interest-convergence', *British Journal of Educational Studies*, 58 (1): 3–25.

Gleeson, D. and Shain, F. (1999) 'Managing ambiguity: between markets and managerialism – a case study of "middle" managers in further education', *The Sociological Review*, 47 (3): 461–90.

Gorard, S. (2012) 'Experiencing fairness at school: an international study', *International Journal of Educational Research*, 53: 127–37.

Gorard, S., Lumby, J., Briggs, A., Morrison, M., Hall, I., Maringe, F., See, B.H., Wright, S. and Shaheen, R. with Corcoran, C., Finbar-Fox, J.J. and Pring, R. (2008) *National Report on the 14–19 Reform Programme: Baseline of Evidence 2007–2008*. Birmingham: University of Birmingham.

Gov.uk (2015) www.gov.uk/children-with-special-educational-needs/overview (accessed 10.04.15).

Grant, C.A. and Portera, C. (eds) (2011) *Intercultural and Multicultural Education*. Abingdon: Routledge.

Grogan, M. and Dias, S (2015) 'Inclusive leadership and gender', in G. Theoharis and M. Scanlan (eds), *Leadership for Increasingly Diverse Schools*. New York: Routledge, pp. 119–41.

Groundhog Day (1993) Motion picture, dir. H. Ramis. Sony Pictures.

GTCS (2012) *Standards for Leadership and Management in Scotland*. Edinburgh: General Teaching Council for Scotland.

Guasp, A., Ellison, G. and Satara, T. (2014) *The Teachers' Report: Homophobic Bullying in Britain's Schools in 2014*. Stonewall. www.stonewall.org.uk/sites/default/files/teachers_report_2014.pdf (accessed 04.05.16).

Guskey, T.R. (2002) 'Does it make a difference? Evaluating professional development', *Educational Leadership*, 59 (6): 45–51. www.ascd.org/publications/educational-leadership/mar02/vol59/num06/Does-It-Make-a-Difference%C2%A2-Evaluating-Professional-Development.aspx (accessed 19.04.15).

Hall, C. and Noyes, A. (2009) 'New regimes of truth: the impact of performative school self-evaluation systems on teachers' professional identities', *Teaching and Teacher Education*, 25 (6): 850–6.

Hallam, S. and Ireson, J. (2003) 'Secondary school teachers' attitudes towards and beliefs about ability grouping', *British Journal of Educational Psychology*, 73 (3): 343–56.

Hallam, S., Ireson, J. and Davies, J. (2004) 'Primary pupils' experiences of different types of grouping in school', *British Educational Research Journal*, 30 (4): 515–33.

Hallam, S. and Parsons, S. (2013) 'Prevalence of streaming in UK primary schools: evidence from the Millennium Cohort Study', *British Educational Research Journal*, 39 (3): 514–44.

Hamill, P. and Boyd, B. (2002) 'Equality, fairness and rights: the young person's voice', *British Journal of Special Education*, 29 (3): 111–17.

Hanushek, E.A. (2006) 'Does educational tracking affect performance and inequality? Differences-in-differences evidence across countries', *The Economic Journal*, 116 (510): C63–C76.

Hartley, R. (2010) *Teacher Expertise for Special Educational Needs: Filling in the Gaps*. London: Policy Exchange. www.policyexchange.org.uk/images/publi cations/teacher%20expertise%20for%20sen%20-%20jul%2010.pdf (accessed 11.10.15).

Harvey, J. and Delfabbro, P.H. (2004) 'Psychological resilience in disadvantaged youth: a critical overview', *Australian Psychologist*, 39 (1): 3–13.

Hatcher, R. (2006) 'Social class and schooling: differentiation or democracy?', in M. Cole (ed.), *Education, Equality and Human Rights: Issues of Gender, Race, Sexuality, Disability and Social Class*. London: Routledge, pp. 202–24

Heineck, G. and Riphahn, R.T. (2007) *Intergenerational Transmission of Educational Attainment in Germany: The Last Five Decades*, Discussion papers, No. 738. Berlin: German Institute for Economic Research. www.diw.de/documents/ publikationen/73/74360/dp738.pdf (accessed 27.04.16)

Henry, M. (2001) *Policy Approaches to Educational Disadvantage and Equity in Australian Schooling*. Paris: UNESCO, International Institute for Educational Planning.

Hirschman, A.O. (1970) *Exit, Voice and Loyalty: Responses to Decline in Firms, Organizations and States*. Cambridge, MA: Harvard University Press.

Hu, G. (2002) 'Potential cultural resistance to pedagogical imports: the case of communicative language teaching in China', *Language Culture and Curriculum*, 15 (2): 93–105.

Hughes, J. (2011) 'Are separate schools divisive? A case study from Northern Ireland', *British Educational Research Journal*, 37 (5): 829–50.

Hull, G., Zacher, J. and Hibbert, L. (2009) 'Youth, risk and equity in a global world', *Review of Research in Education*, 33: 117–59.

Hunt, R. and Jensen, J. (2007) *The School Report: The Experiences of Young Gay People in Britain's Schools*. London: Stonewall.

Hutton, W. (2005) *Where Are the Gaps? An Analysis of UK Skills and Education Strategy in the Light of the Kok Group and European Commission Midterm Review of the Lisbon Goals*. London: Work Foundation/DfES.

Hwang, G.J., Tseng, J.C. and Hwang, G.H. (2008) 'Diagnosing student learning problems based on historical assessment records', *Innovations in Education and Teaching International*, 45 (1): 77–89.

Hyland, T. (2002) 'On the upgrading of vocational studies: analysing prejudice and subordination in English education', *Educational Review*, 54 (3): 287–96.

Iannelli, C. and Smyth, E. (2008) 'Mapping gender and social background differences in education and youth transitions across Europe', *Journal of Youth Studies*, 11 (2): 213–32.

Jackson, C. (2006) *Lads and Ladettes in School: Gender and a Fear of Failure*. Maidenhead: Open University Press.

Jeffrey, B. (2002) 'Performativity and primary teacher relations', *Journal of Education Policy*, 17 (5): 531–46. http://oro.open.ac.uk/20324/1/Performativity_ and_Teacher_Relations.pdf (accessed 20.07.15).

Jenks, C. (1993) *Culture: Key Ideas*. London: Routledge.

Jennett, M. (2004) *Stand Up for Us: Challenging Homophobia in Schools*. Health Development Agency. http://webarchive.nationalarchives.gov.uk/2013040115 1715/http://www.education.gov.uk/publications/eOrderingDownload/SUFU% 20Final.pdf (accessed 23.01.16).

Jensen, E. (2009) *Teaching with Poverty in Mind: What Being Poor Does to Kids' Brains and What Schools Can Do About It*. Alexandria, VA: ASCD.

Kern, V. (2015) 'Child poverty in the EU', Brussels, European Parliamentary Research Service. http://epthinktank.eu/2015/06/09/child-poverty-in-the-eu/ (accessed 20.07.15).

Kristen, C. (2003) *School Choice and Ethnic School Segregation: Primary School Selection in Germany*. Munster: Waxmann Verlag.

Kutner, M. (1992) *Staff Development for ABE and ESL Teachers and Volunteers*. Washington, DC: ERIC Clearinghouse. www.ericdigests.org/1993/abe.htm (accessed 05.05.16).

Ladson-Billings, G. (2006) 'From the achievement gap to the education debt: understanding achievement in US schools', *Educational Researcher*, 35 (7): 3–12.

Larsen, J., Bunting, V. and Armstrong, D. (2011) 'What works? An empirical assessment of strengths, weaknesses and next steps for the academies initiative', *Education Policy and the State: The Academies Programme*. London: Continuum, pp. 105–19.

Leeman, Y.A.M. (2003) 'School leadership for intercultural education', *Intercultural Education*, 14 (1): 31–45.

Legewie, J. and DiPrete, T.A. (2012) 'School context and the gender gap in educational achievement', *American Sociological Review*, 77 (3): 463–85.

Leonard, D. and Murphy, D. (2007) 'Single sex schools', in K. Myers, H. Taylor, S. Adler and D. Leonard, *Genderwatch: Still Watching* ... Stoke on Trent: Trentham Books, pp. 141–3.

Lepkowska, D. (2012) 'Where are the disabled teachers?', *The Guardian*, 12 November.

Levin, B. (2003) *Approaches to Equity in Policy for Lifelong Learning*. Paris: OECD. www.oxydiane.net/IMG/pdf/OECD_Eq_backgr.pdf (accessed 27.04.2016).

Lewis, S. and Starkey, J. (2013) *Ethnic Minority Pupils: Evidence, Review and Practice in Wales*. Cardiff: Welsh Government.

Liasidou, A. and Svensson, C. (2012) 'Theorizing educational change within the context of inclusion', in J. Cornwall and L. Graham-Matheson (eds), *Leading on Inclusion: Dilemmas, Debates and New Perspectives*. London: Routledge, pp. 33–44.

López, G.R., Scribner, J.D. and Mahitivanichcha, K. (2001) 'Redefining parental involvement: lessons from high-performing migrant-impacted schools', *American Educational Research Journal*, 38 (2): 253–88.

López Vilaplana, C. (2013) 'Children at risk of poverty or social exclusion', Eurostat. http://ec.europa.eu/eurostat/statistics-explained/index.php/Children_at_risk_ of_poverty_or_social_exclusion (accessed 14.06.15).

Lugg, C.A. and Tooms, A.K. (2010) 'A shadow of ourselves: identity erasure and the politics of queer leadership', *School Leadership and Management*, 30 (1): 77–91.

Lumby, J. (2007) '14 to 16 year olds in further education colleges: lessons for learning and leadership', *Journal of Vocational Education & Training*, 59 (1): 1–18.

Lumby, J. (2011) 'Enjoyment and learning: policy and secondary school learners' experience in England', *British Educational Research Journal*, 37 (2): 247–64.

Lumby, J. (2012a) 'Disengaged and disaffected young people: surviving the system', *British Educational Research Journal*, 38 (2): 261–79.

Lumby, J. (2012b) 'Leading organisational culture: issues of power and equity', in T. Bush and M. Crawford (eds), *Educational Management, Administration and Leadership*, 40th Anniversary Special Issue, 40 (6): 576–91.

Lumby, J. (2013) 'Longstanding challenges, new contexts: leadership for equality', *International Studies in Educational Administration*, 40 (3): 17–32.

Lumby, J. (2015) 'Women leading South African schools in communities of multiple deprivation', *Educational Management Administration & Leadership*, 43 (3): 400–17.

Lumby, J. with Coleman, M. (2007) *Leadership and Diversity: Challenging Theory and Practice in Education*. London: Sage.

Lumby, J. and Foskett, N. (2011) 'Power, risk and utility – interpreting the landscape of culture in educational leadership', *Education Administration Quarterly*, 47 (3): 446–61.

Lumby, J. and Heystek, H. (2012) 'Leadership identity in ethnically diverse schools in South Africa and England', *Educational Management Administration and Leadership*, 40 (1): 7–23.

Lynch, K. and Baker, J. (2005) 'Equality in education: an equality of condition perspective', *Theory and Research in Education*, 3 (2): 131–64.

Mackenbach, J.P., Menvielle, G., Jasilionis, D. and de Gelder, R. (2015) 'Measuring educational inequalities in mortality statistics', Directorate STD Working Paper No. 66. Brussels: OECD. www.oecd.org/officialdocuments/publicdisplaydocum entpdf/?cote=STD/DOC(2015)8&docLanguage=En (accessed 08.01.16).

Macleod, S., Sharp, C., Bernardinelli, D., Skipp, A. and Higgins, S. (2015) *Supporting the Attainment of Disadvantaged Pupils: Articulating Success and Good Practice*. London: DfE. www.gov.uk/government/uploads/system/uploads/attachment_ data/file/473974/DFE-RR411_Supporting_the_attainment_of_disadvantaged_ pupils.pdf (accessed 30.11.15).

Macpherson, W. (1999) *The Stephen Lawrence Inquiry*. Cm4262-I. www.gov.uk/ government/uploads/system/uploads/attachment_data/file/277111/4262.pdf (accessed 08.05.16).

Magill, K. and Rodriguez, A. (2015) 'Hope, rage and inequality: a critical humanist', *Inclusive Education. International Journal of Progressive Education*, 11 (1): 6–27.

Maguire, M. (2006) 'Gender and movement in social policy', in C. Skelton, B. Francis and L. Smulyan (eds), *The Sage Handbook of Gender and Education*. London: Sage, pp. 109–24.

Martin, A.J. and Marsh, H.W. (2008) 'Academic buoyancy: towards an understanding of students' everyday academic resilience', *Journal of School Psychology*, 46: 53–83.

Mau, A. (2014) 'Beyond kung fu and takeaways? Negotiation of British Chinese identities in schools', in R. Race and V. Lander (eds), *Advancing Race and Ethnicity in Education*. Basingstoke: Palgrave Macmillan, pp. 111–27.

McCormack, M. (2011) 'The declining significance of homohysteria for male students in three sixth forms in the south of England', *British Educational Research Journal*, 37 (2): 337–53.

McEachron, G. and Bhatti, G. (2005) 'Language support for immigrant children: a study of state schools in the UK and US', *Language, Culture and Curriculum*, 18 (2): 164–80.

McLoughlin, C. and Lee, M.J. (2010) 'Personalised and self-regulated learning in the Web 2.0 era: international exemplars of innovative pedagogy using social software', *Australasian Journal of Educational Technology*, 26 (1): 28–43.

McNamara, G. and Norman, J. (2010) 'Conflicts of ethos: issues of equity and diversity in faith-based schools', *Educational Management, Administration and Leadership*, 38 (5): 534–46.

'Mediterranean migrants' (2015) 'Mediterranean migrants: details emerge of deadly capsize', *BBC News*, 21 April. www.bbc.co.uk/news/world-europe-32399433 (accessed 27.11.15).

Meyer, E.J. (2010) *Gender and Sexual Diversity in Schools*. Dordrecht: Springer.

Miller, P. (2011) 'Free choice, free schools and the academisation of education in England', *Research in Comparative and International Education*, 6 (2): 170–82.

Mills, M., Martino, W. and Lingard, B. (2004) 'Attracting, recruiting and retaining male teachers: policy issues in the male teacher debate', *British Journal of Sociology & Education*, 25 (3): 355–69.

Mistry, M. and Sood, K. (2015) 'Why are there still so few men within Early Years in primary schools? Views from male trainee teachers and male leaders', *Education 3–13*, 43 (2): 115–27.

Mitchell, M., Gray, M. and K. Beninger (2014) *Tackling Homophobic, Biphobic and Transphobic Bullying among School Age Children and Young People*. London: NatCen Social Research.

Modood, T. and Calhoun, C. (2015) *Religion in Britain: Challenges for Higher Education*. London: Leadership Foundation.

Morrison, M. and Lumby, J. (2006) *Equal Status Reviews*. Lincoln: University of Lincoln.

Morrison, N. (2014) 'Increase in number of special school pupils reverses trend towards inclusion', *tesconnect*. www.tes.co.uk/news/school-news/breaking-news/increase-number-special-school-pupils-reverses-trend-towards (accessed 03.05.15).

Moskal, M. (2014) 'Polish migrant youth in Scottish schools: conflicted identity and family capital', *Journal of Youth Studies*, 17 (2): 279–91.

Myers, K. and Taylor, H. with Adler, S. and Leonard, D. (2007) *Genderwatch: Still Watching ...* Stoke on Trent: Trentham Books.

NALDIC (2015) 'EAL pupils in schools'. www.naldic.org.uk/research-and-information/eal-statistics/eal-pupils (accessed 23.02.15).

National Union of Teachers (n.d.) *Anti-Semitism in the UK: A Submission to the All-Party Parliamentary Inquiry into Anti-Semitism in the UK from the National*

Union of Teachers. www.teachers.org.uk/files/Anti-Semitism_4424.pdf (accessed 02.11.15).

Newman, K.L. Samimy, K. and Romstedt, K. (2010) 'Developing a training program for secondary teachers of English language learners in Ohio', *Theory into Practice*, 49 (2): 152–61.

Norwich, B. (ed.) (2014) 'A school for the future – 2025: practical futures thinking', *Journal of Research in Special Educational Needs*, 14 (1): 51–65.

Nusche, D. (2009) 'What works in migrant education? A review of evidence and policy options', OECD Education Working Paper No. 22. Paris: OECD.

Oakes, J. (1992) 'Can tracking research inform practice? Technical, normative, and political considerations', *Educational Researcher*, 21: 12–21.

OECD (n.d.) *Inequality and Education.* www.oecd.org/social/inequality.htm#education (accessed 15.11.15).

OECD (2007) *PISA 2006: Science Competencies for Tomorrow's World.* Paris: OECD.

OECD (2009) *OECD Reviews of Migrant Education: Closing the Gap for Immigrant Students: Policies, Practice and Performance.* www.oecd.org/edu/school/oecdreviewsofmigranteducation-closingthegapforimmigrantstudentspoliciespracticeandperformance.htm (accessed 05.05.16).

OECD (2012) *Equity and Quality in Education: Supporting Disadvantaged Students and Schools.* www.oecd.org/education/school/50293148.pdf (accessed 21.07.15).

OECD (2013) *Teaching and Learning International Survey* (TALIS). http://stats.oecd.org/ (accessed 15.11.15).

OECD (2014a) *Education at a Glance 2014: OECD Indicators.* Paris: OECD.

OECD (2014b) *Are Boys and Girls Equally Prepared for Life?* www.oecd.org/pisa/pisaproducts/PIF-2014-gender-international-version.pdf (accessed 06.06.15).

OECD (2015a) *A Closer Look at Gender Gaps in Education and Beyond*, OECD Insights. http://oecdinsights.org/2015/03/05/a-closer-look-at-gender-gaps-in-education-and-beyond/ (accessed 06.06.15).

Ofsted (2006) *Inclusion: Does It Matter Where Pupils Are Taught?* London: Ofsted.

Ofsted (2012) *No Place for Bullying.* Manchester: Ofsted.

Ofsted (2014a) *The Annual Report of Her Majesty's Chief Inspector of Education, Children's Services and Skills 2013/14.* London: HMI.

Ofsted (2014b) *Overcoming Barriers: Ensuring that Roma Children Are Fully Engaged and Achieving in Education.* London: HMI.

Ofsted (2015) *School Inspection Handbook.* Manchester: Ofsted.

Ogunbawo, D. (2012) 'Developing black and minority ethnic leaders: the case for customized programmes', *Educational Management Administration and Leadership*, 40 (2): 158–74.

Ollis, D. (2010) '"I haven't changed bigots but …": reflections on the impact of teacher professional learning in sexuality education', *Sex Education*, 10 (2): 217–30.

O'Nions, H. (2010) 'Different and unequal: the educational segregation of Roma pupils in Europe', *Intercultural Education*, 21 (1): 1–13.

Osler, A. and Starkey, H. (2005) 'Violence in schools and representations of young people: a critique of government policies in France and England', *Oxford Review of Education*, 31: 191–211.

Ossewaarde, M. (2014) 'The national identities of the "death of multiculturalism" discourse in Western Europe', *Journal of Multicultural Discourses*, 9 (3): 173–89.

Oxfam (2010) *The Millennium Development Goals Millennium Development Goal 2*, www.oxfam.org.uk/~/media/Files/Education/Resources/Change%20the%20 world%20in%20eight%20steps/goal_2.ashx (accessed online 16.01.15).

Paechter, P. (2007) *Being Boys Being Girls: Learning Masculinities and Femininities*. Maidenhead: Open University Press.

Panjwani, F. (2014) 'Beyond the saga of the "Trojan horse": some reflections on teaching about Islam in schools', *The Middle East in London*, 10 (5): 9–10.

Parker-Jenkins, M. (2014) 'Identity, belief and cultural sustainability: a case-study of the experiences of Jewish and Muslim schools in the UK', in J.D. Chapman, S. McNamara, M. Reiss and Y. Waghid (eds), *International Handbook of Learning, Teaching and Leading in Faith-Based Schools*. Netherlands: Springer, pp. 157–76.

Paton, G. (2014) 'A-Levels 2014: gender gap between boys and girls closing', *Daily Telegraph*, 21 August.

Patrikios, S. and Curtice, J. (2014) 'Attitudes towards school choice and faith schools in the UK: a question of individual preference or collective interest?', *Journal of Social Policy*, 43 (3): 517–34.

Pearson, S. (2010) 'Narrowing the gap between intention and reality: the case of special educational needs governors in English schools', *Educational Management, Administration and Leadership*, 39 (6): 695–711.

Peske, H. G. and Haycock, K. (2006) *Teaching Inequality: How Poor and Minority Students are Shortchanged on Teacher Quality*. A report and recommendations by the Education Trust. Washington, DC: Education Trust.

Phillips, C., Tse, D., Johnson, F. and Ipsos MORI (2011) *Community Cohesion and PREVENT: How Have Schools Responded?* London: DfE.

Poppleton, S., Hitchcock, K., Lymperopoulou, K., Simmons, J. and Gillespie, R. (2013) *Social and Public Service Impacts of International Migration at the Local Level Research Report 72*. London: Home Office.

Prime Minister's Strategy Unit (2005) *Improving the Prospects of People Living in Areas of Multiple Deprivation in England*. London: Cabinet Office/ODPM.

Quick, D., Lehmann, J. and Deniston, T. (2003) 'Opening doors for students with disabilities on community college campuses: what have we learned? What do we still need to know?', *Community College Journal of Research & Practice*, 27 (9–10): 815–27.

Rawls, J. (1968) 'Distributive justice: some addenda', Natural Law Forum, Paper no. 138. http://scholarship.law.nd.edu/nd_naturallaw_forum/138 (accessed 22.01.16).

Reardon, S.F. (2011) 'The widening academic achievement gap between the rich and the poor: new evidence and possible explanations', in G. J. Duncan and R. J. Murnane (eds), *Whither Opportunity? Rising Inequality, Schools, and Children's Life Chances*. New York: Russell Sage Foundation, pp. 91–116.

Reay, D. (2006) 'The zombie stalking English schools: social class and educational inequality', *British Journal of Educational Studies*, 54 (3): 288–307.

Reay, D. (2010) 'Sociology, social class and education', in M. Apple, S. Ball and L.A. Gandin (eds), *The Routledge Handbook of the Sociology of Education*. London: Routledge. pp. 396–404.

Renold, E. (2000) '"Coming out": gender, (hetero) sexuality and the primary school', *Gender and Education*, 12 (3): 309–26.

Reynolds, G. (2008) 'The impacts and experiences of migrant children in UK Secondary Schools', Working Paper No 47. Brighton: University of Sussex, Sussex Centre for Migration Research, pp. 1–34. www.sussex.ac.uk/webteam/gateway/file.php?name=mwp47.pdf&site=252 (accessed 05.05.16).

Rienzo, C. and Vargas-Silva, C. (2014) *Migrants in the UK: An Overview*. Oxford: Migration Observatory. www.migrationobservatory.ox.ac.uk/briefings/migrants-uk-overview (accessed 17.02.15).

Riley, K., Ellis, S., Weinstock, W., Tarrant, J. and Hallmond, S. (2006) 'Re-engaging disaffected pupils in learning: insights for policy and practice', *Improving Schools*, 9 (1): 17–31.

Ringrose, J., Gill, R., Livingstone, S. and Harvey, L. (2013) 'Teen girls, sexual double standards and "sexting": gendered value in digital image exchange', *Feminist Theory*, 14 (3): 305–23.

Rix, J., Sheehy, K., Fletcher-Campbell, F., Crisp, M. and Harper, A. (2012) 'Exploring provision for children identified with special educational needs: an international review of policy and practice', *European Journal of Special Needs Education*, 28 (4): 375–91.

Rizvi, F. and Lingard, B. (2009) *Globalizing Education Policy*. London: Routledge.

Robeyns, I. (2005) 'The capability approach: a theoretical survey', *Journal of Human Development*, 6 (1): 93–117.

Romanowski, M.H. (2003) 'Meeting the unique needs of the children of migrant farm workers', *The Clearing House*, 77 (1): 27–33.

Ross, A., Hartsmar, N. and Dooly, M. (2012) *Equalities and Education in Europe: Explanations and Excuses for Inequality*. Newcastle upon Tyne: Cambridge Scholars Publishing.

Rubie-Davies, C.M., Peterson, E. and Irving, E. (2010) 'Expectations of achievement: student, teacher and parent perceptions', *Research in Education*, 83 (1): 36–53.

Samaritans (2015) *Suicide Statistics Report, 2015*. www.samaritans.org/sites/default/files/kcfinder/branches/branch-96/files/Suicide_statistics_report_2015.pdf (accessed 15.10.15).

Sandberg, R. (2011) 'A uniform approach to religious discrimination? The position of teachers and other school staff in the UK', in M. Hunter-Henin (ed.), *Law, Religious Freedoms and Education in Europe*. Aldershot: Ashgate, pp. 327–46.

Schaefer, L. (2013) 'Beginning teacher attrition: a question of identity making and identity shifting', *Teachers and Teaching*, 19 (3): 260–74.

Schölmerich, A., Leyendecker, B., Citlak, B., Caspar, U. and Jäkel, J. (2008) 'Assessment of migrant and minority children', *Zeitschrift für Psychologie/Journal of Psychology*, 216 (3): 187.

Sen, A. (1980) *Equality of What?* (Vol. 1, pp. 197–220). www.akira.ruc.dk/~fkt/filosofi/Artikler%20m.m/Egalitarianism/Sen%20-%20Equality%20of%20What.pdf (accessed online 03.02.15).

Sen, A. (1999) *Development as Freedom*. Oxford University Press.

Sen, A. (2012) 'Values and justice', *Journal of Economic Methodology*, 19 (2): 101–8.

Shah, S. (2006) 'Leading multiethnic schools: a new understanding of Muslim youth identity', *Journal of Educational Management, Administration and Leadership*, Special Edition on Leadership and Diversity, 34 (2): 215–37.

Shah, S. and Shaikh, J. (2010) 'Leadership progression of Muslim male teachers: interplay of ethnicity, faith and visibility', *School Leadership and Management*, 30 (1): 19–33.

Shain, F. (2011) *The New Folk Devils: Muslim Boys and Education in England*. Stoke-on-Trent: Trentham Books.

Sherwood, H. (2015) '"She is Jewish, but she's OK" – the primary head minding the faith gaps', *The Guardian*, 11 October. www.theguardian.com/educa tion/2015/oct/11/primary-school-headteacher-faith-gaps-melanie-michael (accessed 29.10.15).

Shields, C.M. (2004) 'Dialogic leadership for social justice: overcoming pathologies of silence', *Educational Administration Quarterly*, 40 (1): 109–32.

Shields, C.M. and Mohan, E.J. (2008) 'High-quality education for all students: putting social justice at its heart', *Teacher Development: An International Journal of Teachers' Professional Development*, 12 (4): 289–300.

Sian, K. P. (2015) 'Spies, surveillance and stakeouts: monitoring Muslim moves in British state schools', *Race Ethnicity and Education*, 18 (2): 183–201.

Singal, N. (2010) 'Including "children with special needs" in the Indian education system: negotiating a contested terrain', in R. Rose (ed.), *Confronting Obstacles to Inclusion*. London: Routledge, pp. 45–57.

Slee, R. (2011) *The Irregular School: Exclusion, Schooling and Inclusive Education*. London: Taylor & Francis.

Slee, R. (2014) 'Evolving theories of student disengagement: a new job for Durkheim's children?', *Oxford Review of Education*, 40 (4): 446–65.

Smith, E. and Gorard, S. (2012) '"Teachers are kind to those who have good marks": a study of Japanese young people's views of fairness and equity in school', *Compare: A Journal of Comparative and International Education*, 42 (1): 27–46.

Sosu, E. and Ellis, S. (2014) *Closing the Attainment Gap in Scottish Education*. York: Joseph Rowntree Foundation.

Stevenson, J. (2012) *Black and Minority Ethnic Student Degree Retention and Attainment*. York: HEA.

Stitzlein, S.M. (2012) *Teaching for Dissent: Citizenship Education and Political Activism*. Boulder, CO: Paradigm.

Stokes, L., Rolfe, H., Hudson-Sharp, N. and Steven, S. (2015) *A Compendium of Evidence on Ethnic Minority Resilience to the Effects of Deprivation on Attainment*, Research report. London: DfE.

Stone, D. and Colella, A. (1996) 'A model of factors affecting the treatment of disabled individuals in organizations', *Academy of Management Review*, 12 (2): 352–401.

Stonewall (undated) *An Introduction to Supporting Lesbian, Gay and Bisexual Young People: A Guide for Schools*. Stonewall. www.stonewall.org.uk/sites/

default/files/an_introduction_to_supporting_lgbt_young_people_-_a_guide_for_schools_2015.pdf (accessed 18.12.15).

Strand, S. (2015) *Ethnicity, Deprivation and Educational Achievement at Age 16 in England: Trends Over Time*. Annex to compendium of evidence on ethnic minority resilience to the effects of deprivation on attainment. London: DfE.

Sullivan, A. (2009) 'Academic self-concept, gender and single sex schooling', *British Educational Research Journal*, 35 (2): 259–88.

Sutton Trust (2013) 'Top comprehensives are more socially selective with only half national average proportion of pupils on free school meals'. www.suttontrust.com/newsarchive/top-comprehensives-socially-selective-half-national-average-proportion-pupils-free-school-meals/ (accessed 15.12.15).

Swann Report (1985) *Education for All: The Report of the Committee of Inquiry into the Education of Children from Ethnic Minority Groups*. London: Her Majesty's Stationery Office.

Szalai, J. (2011) *Ethnic Differences in Education and Diverging Prospects for Urban Youth in an Enlarged Europe*. EDUMIGROM. Budapest: Central European University, Center for Policy Studies.

Teacher Support Network (2014) http://teachersupport.info (accessed 21.05.14).

Terzi, L. (2008) *Justice and Equality in Education*. London: Continuum.

Thompson, D. (2012) 'Whole school development, inclusion and special educational needs', in J. Cornwall and L. Graham-Matheson (eds), *Leading on Inclusion: Dilemmas, Debates and New Perspectives*. London: Routledge, pp. 45–57.

Tissot, S. (2011) 'Excluding Muslim women: from hijab to niqab, from school to public space', *Public Culture*, 23 (1): 39–46.

Torevell, D., Felderhof, M.C. and Thompson, M.P. (eds) (2013) *Inspiring Faith in Schools: Studies in Religious Education*. Aldershot: Ashgate.

Trethewey, A. and Menzies, L. (n.d.) *Encountering Faiths and Beliefs: The Role of Intercultural Education in Schools and Communities*. www.3ff.org.uk/documents/reports/encounteringfaithsbeliefs2015.pdf (accessed 04.05.16).

United Nations General Assembly (1989) *Convention on the Rights of the Child*. www.unicef.org/crc/index.html (accessed 18.01.07).

United Nations General Assembly (2013) *International Migration and Development: Report of the Secretary-General*. www.iom.int/files/live/sites/iom/files/What-We-Do/docs/SG-report-Intl-Migration-and-Development-2013-A_68_190-EN.pdf (accessed 20.02.15).

Valle, J.W., Solis, S., Volpitta, D. and Connor, D.J. (2004). 'The disability closet: teachers with learning disabilities evaluate the risks and benefits of "coming out"', *Equity & Excellence in Education*, 37 (1): 4–17.

van Driel, B. (2004) *Confronting Islamophobia in Educational Practice*. Stoke-on-Trent: Trentham Books.

Vicars, M. (2006) 'Who are you calling queer? Sticks and stones can break my bones, but names will always hurt me', *British Educational Research Journal*, 32 (3): 347–61.

Vincent, C. (2013) *Parents and Teachers: Power and Participation*. London: Routledge.

Vryonides, M. (2014) 'Interethnic violence in schools across European countries', in M. Sedmak, Z. Medaric and S. Walker (eds), *Children's Voices: Studies of Interethnic Conflict and Violence in European Schools.* Abingdon: Routledge, pp. 49–63.

Walker, P. (2015) 'Ofsted targets "growing threat" of unregistered schools', *The Guardian*, 11 December. www.theguardian.com/education/2015/dec/11/ofsted-unregistered-schools-inspectors-faith (accessed 15.12.15).

Ward, R.M. (2014) '"I'm a Geek I am": academic achievement and the performance of a studious working-class masculinity', *Gender in Education*, 26 (7): 709–25.

Ward, S.C., Bagley, C., Lumby, J., Woods, P., Hamilton, T. and Roberts, A. (2015) 'School leadership for equity: lessons from the literature', *International Journal of Inclusive Education*, 19 (4): 333–46.

Warwick, E., Chase, E. and Aggleton, P. (2004) *Homophobia, Sexual Orientation and Schools: A Review and Implications for Action*, Research Report No. 594. Nottingham: DfES.

Weale, S. (2015) 'More than *snopp* and *snippa*: how UK could learn from Swedish sex lessons', *The Guardian*, 6 June.

Webster, R. and Blatchford, P. (2015) 'Worlds apart: the nature and quality of the educational experiences of pupils with a statement for SEN in mainstream primary classrooms', *British Educational Research Journal*, 41 (2): 324–42.

West, A. and Hind, A. (2003) 'Secondary school admissions in England: exploring the extent of overt and covert selection', Centre for Educational Research, Department of Social Policy, London School of Economics and Political Science, Final Report, March. www.risetrust.org.uk/pdfs/admissions.html (accessed 27.04.16).

West, J. and Steedman, H. (2003) *Finding Our Way: Vocational Education in England*. Centre for Economic Performance, London School of Economics and Political Science.

White, R., Sims, D. and Walkey, S. (2014) *NFER Teacher Voice Omnibus Research Report for the Social Mobility and Child Poverty Commission*. London: Social Mobility and Child Poverty Commission.

Wiggins, A. and Tymms, P. (2002) 'Dysfunctional effects of league tables: a comparison between English and Scottish primary schools', *Public Money and Management*, 22 (1): 43–8.

Wilkin, A., Derrington, C., White, R., Martin, R., Foster, B., Kinder, K. and Rutt, S. (2010) *Improving the Outcomes for Gypsy, Roma and Traveller Pupils: Final Report*. London: DfE.

Willms, J.D. (2006) *Learning Divides: Ten Policy Questions About the Performance and Equity of Schools and Schooling Systems*. Montreal: UNESCO Institute for Statistics.

Wrigley, T. and Kalambouka, A. (2012) 'Academies and achievement: setting the record straight'. www.changingschools.org.uk/academiesfolder/acadtitlecontents.pdf (accessed 27.04.16).

Youdell, D. (2004) 'Identity traps or how Black students fail: the interactions between biographical, sub-cultural and learner identities', in G. Ladson-Billings and D. and Gillborn (eds), *The RoutledgeFalmer Reader in Multicultural Education*. London: RoutledgeFalmer, pp. 84–102.

Younger, M. and Warrington, M. (2005) *Raising Boys' Achievement in Secondary Schools*. Maidenhead: Open University Press.

Zimmer-Gembeck, M.J. and Locke, E.M. (2007) 'The socialization of adolescent coping behaviours: relationships with families and teachers', *Journal of Adolescence*, 30 (1): 1–16.

Index